£1.50

Pike Fishing in the 80's

Pike Fishing in the 80's
Neville Fickling

Beekay Publishers

Also by Beekay Publishers:
Carp Fever by Kevin Maddocks
Success with the Pole by Dickie Carr
Basic Carp Fishing by Peter Mohan
Modern Specimen Hunting by Jim Gibbinson
Fishing for Big Chub by Peter Stone
Top Ten edited by Bruce Vaughan
Redmire Pool by Kevin Clifford & Len Arbery
Cypry the Carp by Peter Mohan
Tactics for Big Pike by Bill Chillingworth
In Pursuit of Carp & Catfish by Kevin Maddocks
The Beekay Guide to Carp Waters
In Pursuit of Predatory Fish by Neville Fickling
Jim Davidson Gets Hooked! by Jim Davidson

(All titles available direct from the publishers.
Send for free catalogue listing more than 200.)

First published 1982
Second edition 1983
Reprinted 1986
BEEKAY PUBLISHERS
Withy Pool
Bedford Road
Henlow Camp
Beds. SG16 6EA
© Neville Fickling 1982
Printed and bound by
Castle Cary Press Limited, Castle Cary, Somerset
ISBN 0 9507598 3 X (hardback)
0 9507598 4 8 (softback)

CONTENTS

Front cover:
The author with a 31.14 Irish pike. Transparency courtesy of Andy Barker.

Back cover:
The author with a nice brace weighing 15 and 12 pounds.

Acknowledgements

My thanks to the contributors to this book, without whose help it would not have been possible: Trevor Moss, Pete Melbourne, George Higgins and Barrie Rickards. Andy Barker and Bruno Broughton provided additional photographs, Pete Melbourne kindly printed the photographs, while the chore of correcting the manuscript fell upon my wife Kathy. A special thanks to all those who have had to put up with me on the bank, notably Hugh and Dickie Reynolds, Basil Chilvers, John McAngus, the Davies family, the Greenacre Gang, Dave and Ben Moore, Dave Phillips, and anyone else I've fished with. Sincere thanks to Kevin Maddocks, head of Beekay Publishers, for the opportunity to write this book. Finally I'd like to acknowledge the biggest influence on my formative days as a pike angler, Barrie Rickards and Ray Webb, not forgetting of course Mr Harry Nelson from the very early days.

The publishers would like to thank Brian Mills whose drawings appear on pages 32, 58, 126, 133 and 145. All other drawings are by the author.

PREFACE TO THE SECOND EDITION

Lucky is the man who can write the foreword to a second edition, for it means that the book is not destined to disappear into obscurity. In order to keep things that way, I have made suitable alterations and additions in a number of places. Though there have been no drastic changes in pike fishing thinking in the last year, the personal process of learning continues, and I hope that I will in this second edition be able to pass on some of this learning.

Neville Fickling
June 1983
Gainsborough

22.05 Reservoir pike.

Introduction

An introduction is probably the most difficult part of a fishing book to write. One is supposed to lead the reader through a little of the subject's history and then show where the author fits into the scheme of things. Presumably one then tells the reader why the author is specially qualified to write in detail on this particular subject. Fishing books present one particular problem in this respect. It is essential to show the reader that the writer has caught good numbers of big fish, but preferably without making the introduction seem like an auction list at Sotheby's! One also has to try and avoid the inevitable ego trip which many of us are tempted to fall for.

Pike fishing has recently become a very popular pursuit, though pike angling has been enjoyed by many of our ancestors over the decades. We will probably find little to interest us in pike angling's early days and it is not until comparatively recently that writers on the subject of pike fishing have conveyed facts rather than fantasies to the reader. Some of the earlier writers such as J. W. Martin, Bickerdyke and Hampton, introduced new ideas to pike fishermen, such as the use of plugs and pike preservation. However it was not until 1965 that Geoffrey Bucknall's book 'Big Pike' was published. From then onwards pike fishing moved ahead in leaps and bounds. Some superb books appeared, particularly those by Rickards and Webb and Martin Gay. Not only did pike angling become more sophisticated, it also became more popular until today when it is said to be the second most popular individual freshwater fish species in the country. This book in no way supersedes any of the aforementioned books, indeed it would be pretentious to think that any new book on pike fishing could rise to such lofty heights. However I hope that this book can perhaps complement and in places update these earlier works, for there is little doubt that some new thinking has occurred during recent years and equally the methods used to catch pike have been modified and perhaps in a small way improved. My own pike fishing background is a varied one. I caught my first pike in 1963 and from then it took another 3 years before I landed my first double. The first twenty pounder followed in 1968 and since then it has given me much pleasure to continue to catch such fish. At the time of writing (March 1983) my total of twenty pounders stands at 71, with 476 double figure pike netted. These are, for me at least, pleasing statistics, but not of course the be all and end all of my pike fishing. I enjoy catching pike of any shape and size, but I also enjoy 'collecting' big pike. To me totals of big fish are interesting and some indication of the angler's seriousness towards his fishing. A big total of specimen pike does not offer a guarantee of the angler's ability, for in many ways I fail to shape up to the popular image of an 'expert' angler. However I believe that I put a fair amount of thought into my pike fishing and more than a fair amount of effort. This gets the desired results so my ability to cast, do fancy tricks with a plug or my proficiency at bait catching are really irrelevant.

Pike, then, are my number one priority and though I will fish for other fish, particularly during the summer, most of my efforts are directed towards pike. For me the pike season usually starts in September and ends in March. About the end of April I have a week's spring pike fishing in Scotland or Ireland. Very rarely do I venture out pike fishing in the summer proper, but now and again I have a whirl with lures, when conditions are favourable. I enjoy fishing any type of pike water and over the years have fished all the different types of waters available in the British Isles. In my formative years as a pike angler the Fen drains were my stamping grounds, but in later years stillwaters have come more and more to the fore, so much so that all my pike over twenty-five pounds have come from reservoirs, lochs, lakes or gravel pits. This does not mean that I have foresaken Fenland drains altogether. I still fish these waters though perhaps spend my time on a wider variety of waters than previously. Fishing a wide variety of waters around the country also means that meetings with other pike anglers are unavoidable. There is little doubt that being in contact with other pike anglers is the best way to learn new methods and waters. I am not by nature one of the world's most creative anglers and certainly require contact with other perhaps more inventive minds to improve my methods of pike fishing. Where I have been influenced by other pike anglers I will mention it in the text. The apparent name dropping is much more than this, being an acknowledgement of those other anglers' influence on my pike fishing.

I hope this book will prove to be both informative and also interesting. The aim has been to describe the methods I use to catch pike, suitably interspersed with accounts of notable days and exceptional fish. Here and there 'guest appearances' by other anglers fill in the gaps in my pike fishing experiences. I cannot honestly say that my way of fishing is the 'best' way to fish for pike, if there is such a thing, however my approach seems to satisfy nearly all of the other catchers of big pike, so it will probably work for you too!

1 Beginnings

The early days of my piking career seem rather blurred now. Though still a few years off middle age, 22 years is a long time to think back and remember even for a relative youngster such as myself. Still, memories are there, not memories of catching pike, at least not at first, but memories of watching pike in their natural environment and spending summer days dabbling with a pond net after sticklebacks and roach fry. Once in a while the chance of a young pike would come along and such chances were the event of the week. Seldom was it possible to capture the pike, the pencil-like shapes always seeming to dissolve away or dart off in a cloud of mud, yet once or twice a year a success came and the satisfaction of the capture was inevitably followed by the return of the 'pikelet' to whence it came, perhaps a little wiser for its experience.

A six foot spinning rod and a tiny centre pin reel saw my introduction to fishing proper. After several years of catching most of the smaller fish species (despite the thick green fishing line!) I graduated to a spinning reel, an Intrepid Envoy if my memory serves me well. The chance to tackle the pike had at last arrived, so armed with a copper Mepps I accompanied father to a small drain near Middle Drove in the depths of Fenland. There he had found the 'Forty Foot Drain' (no relation to the Ramsey Forty Foot) while building a house nearby. The drain reputedly held a forty pound pike and with this in mind we set to work. I fished my spinner while dad sat tight and fished a sprat, the directions for fishing this having been obtained from the Daily Mirror. The Mirror's advice proved worthless, but further up the drain something slammed into my retrieved spinner, and a few minutes later a 1¼lb pike had been unhooked, weighed, photographed and admired. I had begun!

Progress with spinners was rather slow and despite visits to the almost virginal Relief Channel in 1963, pike were slow to accept the fact that I was a budding Dennis Pye. The papers were full of Dennis and his exploits; not surprisingly, at that time he was many a youngster's hero, and I was no exception. Spinning trips on the Relief Channel were always full of surprises, for the perch which abounded there then would frequently follow the lure right to the bank. Some big perch were caught by other anglers, but I had to make do with two small roach foul hooked in the side! There were so many fish in the water at the time that such

Spinning on Fenland's Forty Foot Drain in 1963, shortly after the fateful capture of that first pike.

events were not uncommon. The next trip to the Forty Foot Drain saw me equipped with a large home-made balsa pike bung. Its shape was almost obese and its garish colouration of red and silver would probably have evoked a predatory response from the pike, without seeing the livebait. I proceeded to livebait in the then accepted manner, four feet deep and allowed to swim around. My two livebaits were both about 4 ounces, a dace and a roach. The roach had searched out the water for several hours without attracting the attention of a pike, so I wandered down the bank to see how my dad was doing. Typically the float decided to steam off down the drain just as I had reached dad's spot. Running

The first double of 17½lb from Magdalen Bridge on the Relief Channel in 1966. It also proves that I was not always ugly!

back, I was amazed to see the float running along just beneath the surface and wasted no time grabbing the rod and striking. The next few seconds passed all too quickly; I pulled, the pike pulled, dad said, 'Hold the fish, don't let it go', and I did! Crack—the 13lb line snapped like the proverbial piece of cotton and I said goodbye to what was probably my first double figure pike.

A couple more years of apprenticeship passed and each year my personal best pike increased in size. By the beginning of the 1966 season I had caught pike to 4½lb from the Relief Channel on home-made spoons and had come to terms with livebaiting, once I had bought a 9 foot Japanese rod made by Anon-Shaw known as the Leger-Pike. It cost me 5 guineas' worth of strawberry picking money, but was going to repay that investment amply in the next few years. This rod was to all intents and purposes a shorter version of many of the very popular pike rods we use today; a bit like a North Western SS6. Not surprisingly it made a very good pike rod and could throw anything up to a small whole mackerel a respectable distance.

It was October, and I had discovered Magdalen Bridge on the Relief Channel. Around this bridge throughout the late summer and early autumn resided a huge shoal of fish, with just about every species common in the Relief Channel there for the taking. It was quite easy to catch baits off the bridge, by float fishing a couple of maggots and watching the bait disappear. The only problem came when a good fish was hooked, since then you had to walk the fish to the other side of the bridge and get down to the bank yourself, or if you were lucky get a friend to net the fish. What started out as a bit of fun soon developed into a case of serious pike fishing. Most days while tiddler snatching a pike would put in an appearance, grabbing a fish as it was about to be drawn out of the water. The outcome was always the same—the pike bit through the line. So in October I cycled to Magdalen, caught some bait off the bridge and set about catching some pike. Success was almost immediate, with fish of up to six pounds soon landed. The method was simple, either fishing a livebait under a fixed float down the reedbeds by the bridge, or increasing the depth and fishing further out. It was a few weeks later that I met someone who was going to set me on the road to pike fishing proper. Harry Nelson still lives in Magdalen, although he rarely pike fishes these days. In 1966, however, Harry was making some big hauls of pike from the channel, with the odd twenty pounder thrown in for good measure. His main method was either to floatfish rudd live-baits off the reedbeds or to leger a smelt, caught the day before in the tidal Ouse. The first day I watched him using smelt baits he landed an

My third and biggest twenty by November 1963: 23 pounds exactly.

eighteen pounder, which he quickly returned. Even in those days some anglers cared for the conservation of pike stocks.

Harry helped me with my methods and we often went bait catching on the same water at Gourboulds lake. There in an afternoon we could catch an ample supply of small rudd. Because my casting ability still left a lot to be desired, I persisted with my bridge fishing. Finally one November day in 1966 I cracked it; fishing off the bridge I quickly caught two six pounders. However, I was soon distracted from my reedbed swim by a big swirl in mid channel, directly under the bridge. I upped the depth to 10 feet and dropped a live rudd down to where I hoped the pike was waiting. Nothing much happened until lunch time when the float slid away and decided to go under the bridge. After a great deal of confusion, I eventually walked a large pike across to the other side of the bridge where Harry gaffed it for me. She weighed 17½ pounds, a pleasing start for any youngster and, needless to say, I went the whole hog and made sure it appeared in all the local papers, including, of course, Angling Times and Anglers' Mail. From that day onwards Magdalen became rather more popular than before. If only I had known the way of the world! Still the day had not finished yet and I went on to get another almost identical fish, but not the same fish of 17 pounds. I did not catch another double until 1968! Those early days seemed so incredibly easy and it always seems as if the pike were far more numerous in those days. I sometimes wonder what my results would have been like if I had been able to fish in those days in the same manner as I do today. Fortunately I think that the passing of time tends to make things appear to be much better than they actually were. Even in the mid sixties there were some very good anglers fishing the Relief Channel. Despite this, though their results were very good, these were to improve considerably in later years. Though I may have missed this early period in Fenland pike fishing and also of course missed out completely on the Horsey and Hickling boom period, I feel lucky to have arrived in time to sample really superb pike fishing in many other waters.

2 About the Pike

During the past decade there have been some very interesting books and articles in the press about the pike. The depth to which the author has delved into the pike's habits and biology varies. Fred Buller has probably given the fullest account of aspects of the biology of pike, in his three books on pike, namely: 'Pike', 'The Domesday Book of Mammoth Pike' and 'Pike and the Pike Angler'. Fred's greatest contribution must have been his documenting some really huge pike and in many cases providing convincing photographic evidence. For greater detail about the biology of the pike one really has to consult the scientific literature, although time and time again I have found that the pike angler's best guide is a practical working knowledge of the pike's behaviour as relating to fishing. You do not really need to know exactly how many eggs a female pike can lay or how much food a pike eats in a year! This is the sort of information that is of interest, but not vital to pike fishing success. Some of the best pike anglers are ordinary people who are into the ways of the fish. A degree in Zoology is therefore not essential. For those with an interest in the biology of the pike I have included a list of useful references at the end of the book.

It is a little sad to have to start off by being derisive about the mental capabilities of the pike. Unfortunately it is true that the pike is not particularly bright and there is certainly very little evidence to suggest that it can associate a particular bait with being captured, unless that bait or method has been used intensively. Even then a lot of anglers experiences of a bait going off are due to the pike having long since moved off themselves to pastures new! Pike certainly wise up to artificial lures very quickly, but then this is hardly surprising as most lures are nothing like fish. Live and deadbaits are a different matter and these days I tend to consider the possibility of pike 'wising up to' either, as being so rare as to be nothing to worry about. It is often the angler that loses faith in a method rather than the pike going off it! However just because I think that pike are fairly unintelligent, don't let me close your mind to any possibilities that pike might react adversely to being fished for. An open mind is far better than a closed one. Being able to react to, and assimilate, new information rapidly is a vital requirement of any angler whether he is a match, pleasure or specimen-seeking angler.

A beautifully marked Loch Lomond pike of 7lbs which has unusually retained its juvenile
bar markings.

One thing which is a proven fact is that pike do not like the sight or sound of human beings. Years of evolution in an often hostile environment has taught the pike that humans clumping along the bank invariably means trouble. I doubt if it is coincidence that big pike seldom show themselves on most waters, while their smaller, perhaps less wise brethren are frequently to be seen in shallow water. So when fishing for pike it pays to be reasonably quiet in one's approach to the water and the general rule must be to exercise increasing caution, the smaller the water and the nearer to the fish you are. For very narrow rivers and drains, this may mean precautions which appear at first to be excessive, but which on further thought seem quite reasonable. There is little doubt that pike can detect our presence at 20 yards in clear water, by both sight and vibrations conveyed to the lateral line. Though the pike may not always bolt straightaway, often the next slight move (usually as you cast a bait at it) scares the fish off. At other times the pike just slopes off very gently, fading away before casually swimming off to another area. A spooked pike is also less likely to feed so it is obviously very important to make sure that the pike in your swim are not scared stiff!

Throughout a year pike tend to follow a fairly predictable pattern of behaviour. For about nine months of the year they tend to range far and wide, keeping to the water around 6 to 20 feet deep. During March, April and May (sometimes earlier or later), pike move into very shallow water, first to spawn and shortly after to feed on all the other fish species which enter the shallows to spawn, particularly—and in this order—perch, roach, bream and rudd. While on the shallows the pike pick off the other fish and can consume up to 60% of the annual food ration during a few months. Obviously this is of little use to the majority of English pike anglers, but those of us who make our annual trips to Scotland and Ireland in the spring certainly appreciate that the pike's feeding spree makes for some of the easiest pike fishing of the year.

For the rest of the year pike in nearly all waters lead a fairly mobile life. It was not realised until some of us tagged pike or learned to recognise individual fish that the pike would move long distances. My first experience of this was on the Middle Level in 1973. Here a tagged pike moved about a mile downstream, moved a few hundred yards further down and then changed its mind and moved all the way back past its original capture point to end up a mile further upstream! Such experiences have been repeated on many, many waters and it is almost an accepted fact that pike can and will move long distances over varying periods of time. The most notable study of pike so far conducted along

these lines was by Gerry White and Rosalind Wright on Staunton Harold
Reservoir. Using sonic tags they were able to follow the pike at a discreet
distance and note their movements. One pike moved from the deep
water near the dam to the spawning shallows in less than a day, despite
having remained static for some time. This simply shows that pike
fishing can be very much a case of here today, gone tomorrow!

Pike also frequently return to certain areas on a regular basis. One
particular pike I caught from Loch Lomond had been caught the year
previously from the same bay. Lomond is about 22 miles long and quite
big enough to lose the odd 26 pound pike, yet that fish had returned to
the same area rather than choosing any other. On Lake Windermere
they found the same sort of behaviour with pike tending to return to
similar areas for spawning. Whether this applies to pike in smaller
waters with more widespread spawning areas is unclear, but it is noticeable that the fish are fairly predictable in many waters and it may be
reasonable to assume that once they have spawned or fed in a certain
area, they will do so again at some later date, provided of course conditions remain favourable.

The image of a mobile hunting pike does not perhaps fit in well with
the oft quoted ambush type method of feeding. The classic idea of the
pike being a lazy ambush merchant is in some ways a long way from the
truth. I believe that pike combine hunting and ambush together. First
find the food fish, then position somewhere out of the way, then, first
chance you get, whoosh, grub up! A pike would take a long time to grow
big sitting round waiting for the food to show up. In fact after a while the
food fish would obviously avoid the pike's ambush area like the plague,
so the pike goes out hunting. In really large waters such as the lochs and
loughs of Scotland and Ireland, this has probably led to the pike there
evolving as long sleek predators, with well-toned muscles to enable
constant hunting for prey. Loch pike certainly appear to have larger tail
fins and pectorals than their relatives from smaller English waters. A
similar situation prevails in rivers, where pike can actually be noted
hunting and then resting at a suitable ambush point. This hunting habit
can be most disconcerting as one mate of mine found while he was roach
fishing. A big pike swam by close to the bank in front of him during the
evening and he had no pike tackle!

Another aspect of the pike's biology of more than passing interest
to the pike angler is the rate of growth. It is unfortunate that information
regarding the growth rate of pike can be so very misleading, otherwise
such information would provide us with all we needed to enable the
tracking down of a super pike. A pike can grow to thirty pounds in ten

years or eighteen years, depending on the type of water. A lot depends also on who examines the scales! Pike scales are notoriously difficult to read and it is quite possible (indeed I expect it) to be one or two years out either way. Opercular bones are much better, provided the pike already happens to be dead, since no-one in their right mind goes around killing big pike just to remove the operculum for age determination. The photograph shows an opercular bone with the annuli (zones of slowed winter growth) marked for clarity. Another photograph shows a scale from a very old Hornsea Mere pike and the difficulty in making an age estimate can be appreciated here.

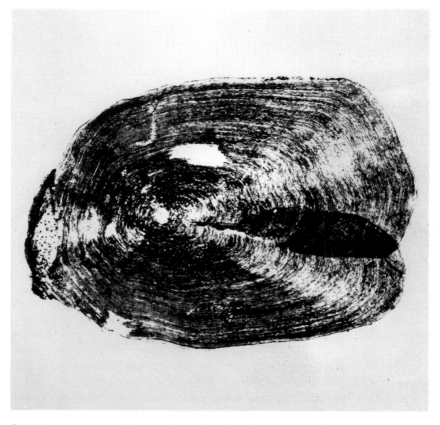

Scale from a ten pound Hornsea Mere pike. I would not try to age a pike precisely from such a scale. The pike was probably slow growing, thus accounting for the difficulty in discerning annuli.

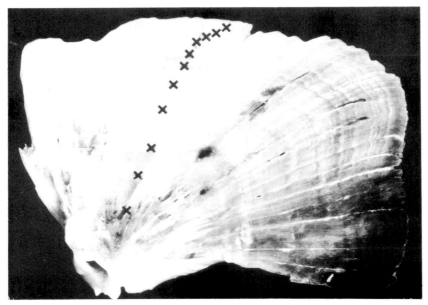

Pike opercular bone showing annuli (crosses). This fish was eleven, perhaps twelve, years old.

Going back to the age of thirty pound pike, the reason why such fish can show differences in age of up to 8 years is easily found. In some waters pike grow very rapidly indeed, usually to a maximum weight of around 32 to 33 pounds. Once this size has been reached, only an exceptional water can provide sufficient food to allow continued growth. It seems that the effort required to obtain food now equals the energy derived from the effort. The pike therefore remains at that weight for a few years and perhaps in some cases drops back to a lower weight. In many waters such pike get caught and are killed. This is particularly true of trout waters. I have often thought that such fast-growing pike are also short-lived. The comparison between the rainbow trout and the brown trout immediately comes to mind. A rainbow grows fast for 4 years then usually dies. A brown trout grows more slowly, but can live for nearly 20 years. Pike are, I believe, similar. In a good but not exceptional water a pike can grow for 18 years and then reach 30 pounds. Though no bigger than the fast-growing fish, the slower-growing thirty has contributed just as much to the pike fishery, yet if we assumed that rapid growth was essential for large size, such waters might have been written off prematurely.

Some recent big pike have been relatively young and this backs up what I have been saying, particularly regarding trout waters. The biggest authenticated English pike of 1981, a 36lb 10oz specimen, was 12 plus years of age according to ex-Grafham bailiff Keith Fisher, while Bruno Broughton's 34¼lb pike from Shropshire was also fairly young at 13 plus. That pike can stop growing and continue to exist, just like carp, has also been proved beyond doubt. I have records of several known fish which have failed to show additional scale growth, despite a year elapsing between captures. Furthermore some pike seem to be able to hang on for years without showing significant growth. One pike of 16¾lb caught by myself had attached to its jaw a tag fitted seven years previously when the pike weighed 16lb and measured ½ inch less. The incredibly detailed scales of pike from Hornsea Mere suggest that some pike have been around for very long periods of time. All of this goes against the scientist's suggestion that as many as 50% of the fish population die each year. This may well be true of pike populations which are being exploited, i.e. pike are being killed and removed from the fishery. However if fish are being returned regularly, it is likely that the recruitment of more pike into the population is reduced due to predation by the larger adults. A shortage of food for the younger fish can also lead to a fairly static population of older fish. Such situations have been noted with zander and it is likely that this can also happen to pike populations. It is a pity that scientific research has not delved into this important area, for suppositions can never be taken as valid when compared with correctly analysed scientific data.

Talking of scientific research brings me onto a particular interest of my own, that of the markings of pike. I cannot say that I was the first person to notice that the spot markings of pike were characteristic of individual fish. However I have made a study of the subject and recently published a scientific paper on The Identification of Pike by Means of Characteristic Marks (see references). Having compared photos of 187 different pike, all from the same side and having concluded that none were similar, it was suggested that all pike have distinctive and unique spot patterns. Having now looked at a lot more than 187 pike by the time of writing this I am as convinced as one can be that the suggestion made above is in fact correct. By the same token, if the photographs of two pike suspected as being the same fish are compared, similarities should immediately become apparent. This is, in fact, the case. Though the spot markings of pike change as they grow (spots are added, but do not necessarily get bigger) my observations have indicated that it is possible to identify pike of over 500mm which have shown percentage length increases of 5.4% and percentage weight increases of 31.3%, over a period of two years.

The best areas to use for identification purposes are the tail root, anal fin, head, behind the gill cover and along the lower body where the spots often break up into a variety of irregular shapes. I usually aim to look for three similar marks in different areas before establishing that the 'two' fish are in fact one and the same. Obviously if all three areas are dissimilar then the two fish are different fish. By the way, the markings on each side of the same fish also differ, so do not try comparing two fish from transparencies with one the wrong way round!

There are often other features unique to individual pike which obviate the need to use the spot pattern for identification purposes. Many pike have the familiar yellow blotches at various points on their bodies. These primrose coloured 'birth marks' can be found just about anywhere and though it is possible that two similar-sized pike from the same water could have the same mark in the same position it is unlikely. Other marks such as scars, fin deformities and parrot or kyped jaws are all fairly rare and can be used to identifiy specific fish. Angler-induced damage can also make a fish easily identifiable, particularly the most unsightly of angler damage, the gaff wound. Even the correctly-used

The Hunchback of the River Delph. Just one of the many deformities which pike suffer from. This one weighed 9lb.

A Concorde pike! Complete with 'droop snoot', this fish weighed 11 pounds, but had I lost it I would have been tempted to think I had lost a 'twenty'.

gaff causes some damage and this remains apparent for at least a year. More careless work with this potentially lethal device can leave the tongue protruding through the lower jaw. I have had several such fish of up to 20 pounds from two different waters and can assure you that it is a most unpleasant sight.

Being able to identify pike leads inevitably to the subject of multiple captures of pike. Like carp anglers, pike specialists have become aware of the fact that pike are often caught several times during their lives. I think it would be safe to say that the smaller the water and the more intensively fished it is, the more frequent are multiple recaptures. I think it was Dave Steuart in the now defunct 'Angling' magazine and Jerry Stapylton in 'Coarse Fisherman' that first really brought this home to pike anglers. Since then pike anglers have paid much more attention to their fish and on certain waters the situation has been reached where all the pike in the water are now 'known' fish. I have heard some people say that this detracts from the fun of fishing a water. While it is true that much of the mystery attached to fishing for pike is removed, the element of not knowing precisely what lurks under the water being important to many anglers, I feel that this is compensated for by the added interest obtained from being able to follow the progress of specific fish year in

Parrot beaked pike are fairly common in Ireland, but seldom encountered in England. T'.is one held by Barry Kerslake weighed 17.05.

year out. It is also very satisfying to know that the angling efforts of yourself and fellow anglers are not affecting the survival and growth of pike in the fishery.

The question I am most interested in answering is, 'How many times can a pike be caught and returned?'. Having kept records on certain waters since 1978, I think I can go some way to answering this question. The all-time record on one fishery I spend some time on, a small gravel pit, is 21 captures in 4 seasons of fishing. This particular fish, nicknamed 'Lumpy' because of the large tumour-like growth attached to its jaw, has been caught repeatedly by a number of anglers, usually at around 13 or 14 pounds, but sometimes going down to just under 12 pounds and sometimes weighing up to 15 pounds. The lump in its mouth probably makes feeding difficult thus accounting for its frequent visits to the bank to be unhooked and put back yet again. A couple of fish in this water put in about half of 'Lumpy's' 'bank time', while the remaining handful of fish very rarely put in an appearance. There are some fish in this pit which have turned up only three times in the four seasons' fishing and who knows if there might be the odd fish left which has yet to appear. There is little doubt that different pike differ in their susceptibility to angling. Some are real suckers while others are very hard to catch indeed. Why this should be is a mystery to me. There seems no relationship between size and ease of capture, once weights of 12 pounds and over are reached. In some waters I fish there are mug twenties and hard doubles. In other waters the situation is reversed. Sometimes the hard and easy fish reverse roles and this inevitably adds to the confusion. Assuming that both easy and hard pike require similar amounts of food to show similar amounts of growth, perhaps the mug fish frequents areas where it is bound to get caught. Perhaps it hunts over a wider area. The harder fish perhaps keeps further out or perhaps feeds at night? On the other hand it is possible that some pike are like human beings. For example some humans suffer from overactive thyroid glands. This causes increased activity, a higher metabolic rate and consequently a faster burning up of energy. A pike in this physiological condition would obviously spend more time swimming and feeding, causing it to get caught more often. The converse would presumably be true for the less active pike with a lower metabolic rate. Perhaps the cause of the mug fish phenomena is a combination of both factors? One thing is certain, because we can seldom if ever stalk our quarry as the carp angler does, we can do little to increase our chances of contacting the more difficult fish, except for fishing more hours and trying to fish when conditions are most favourable. In this way the

The famous Lumpy! Captured at least 21 times in three years, this grotesque growth made feeding difficult, and caused it to be captured repeatedly. The growth was removed at one stage but grew back.

chances of the difficult fish encountering our baits is increased. Whether it takes them or not is a different matter.

I can hear the reader asking now, 'Perhaps the difficult fish have been caught a couple of times and wised up?'. Nice as this theory might seem, it just does not make sense. The very definition of a difficult fish tells us that it has seldom been caught, full stop. Mug fish however get caught regularly and do not seem to learn at all quickly. Does this suggest that one fish is more intelligent than another? Perhaps there is a possibility that the mug fish possess a few less neurones in their skulls, however I am convinced that the physiology of the fish is so dominant over its mental powers (which must be very limited and mainly confined to instinctive rather than learned behaviour) that learning, should I say negative conditioning, is of little importance. I think it fair to say that a mug fish can eventually cease to be a mug fish by changing its behaviour. For instance the Ravensthorpe pike, on being transferred to Hollowell Reservoir, were fairly easy to catch on paternostered livebaits, quite close to the dam. The native fish, on the other hand, seemed much keener on small deadbaits punched out to around 80 yards. However, the following season, both native and introduced pike spent much more time well away from the bank. By 1981 all the pike seemed to be behaving similarly and no significant difference between the large introduced fish and the smaller native fish could be noticed. Both kept well out from the dam a lot of the time and both fell to long range deadbaits and, when boats were out on the water, large livebaits. Circumstantial evidence would suggest that these pike moved away from the dam because of angling pressure. However it could also be true that the native pike knew the best areas to feed in, while the introduced fish had to get to know their new home. The introduced fish would initially be caught nearer to the dam than usual, but once they came to terms with the new environment, they too would react and live like the native fish.

There is a lot more one could say about the pike's reaction to our presentations of various baits. Significance could be attached to finicky runs, lack of runs and the general fall off in catches after a water has been 'hammered'. An in-depth look at these problems is better read in conjunction with the description of methods and will not be pursued further at this point.

Having considered multiple recaptures of pike it is perhaps worthwhile considering the opposite situation, those which have never been captured. It is almost a fact that many of the biggest pike caught in this country, or indeed the world, have only been caught once. If they had been caught previously, few have put the earlier and later capture together and referred to it. Most really big pike invariably get killed. Though this is less likely to be the case in England these days, it is almost always the case in other countries. Even when returned, fish like Clive Loveland's Knipton 39 pounder and Peter Hancock's Horsey 40 pounder did not appear again. (Hancock's fish had little chance thanks to *Prymnesium.*) It seems that a super pike of 35 pounds and over is often the product of a lightly fished water, or an encounter with fate for some lucky angler. The larger the water, the less chance a pike has of being caught. Similarly the more private and exclusive a water, the better the chances of a big pike growing to a huge size. All this depends, of course, on the food supply being sufficient. Ample food supplies generally mean a wide selection of prey sizes and plenty of them. It is hard to be absolutely certain, but it seems that nearly all pike of over 35 pounds have come from very rich waters with lots of bream, trout or migratory trout and salmon passing through them. Some have all these fish! The beauty of migratory fish runs is that they provide an influx of protein which the lake, river, loch, or whatever would have been hard pressed to produce itself. This natural bonus is reproduced to some extent in some of our trout waters.

Migratory fish do not of course include just the salmon and seatrout. In the Fens it is quite common to get big runs of smelt and lampreys which are eaten quite avidly by pike. It used to be fairly common to note half-digested lampreys in pike throats while fishing on the Relief Channel in winter. Flounders and mullet also like to wander into freshwater. On their way upstream and downstream elvers and eels of course fall prey to pike. I have lost count of the fresh and not so fresh eels I have found in pike throats. All these migratory fish add to the pike's larder. Obviously in enclosed waters, migratory fish do not occur, although in rich and mature lakes, gravel pits and reservoirs, where bream are particularly prolific, pike can grow very big. I do not think the size of the prey is quite as important as the density of the prey. The ideal to my mind is a very high density of prey fish of 4 ounces up to two pounds. Some of our better match waters which are stuffed with bream, chub and tench fall into this category. The wide size range enables a pike to grow rapidly from its early days and reach its maximum size as quickly as possible. Rapid growth can be equated with reduced chance of capture before maximum size is reached and I feel that this is very important in all but unfished waters. A pike can convert about 5 pounds of prey to one pound of its own body flesh. Admittedly some of this is lost each spring as spawn, but it is still clear that a pike does not have to eat that much to reach a colossal size. An average of 20 pounds of prey a year might see a 40 pounder in ten years, and so, in theory, a 50 pounder is not beyond the realms of possibility. The records from the past confirm that such fish have been caught, perhaps some even bigger. Unfortunately none seem to have come from the British Isles and Ireland recently. I think the reason for this is a combination of climatic changes, increased pollution of our fisheries and increased angling pressure and culling on waters likely to produce a super pike. Still, somewhere in some untouched corner, who knows? In the meantime we must all come back down to earth and learn to accept that we will be lucky men if we catch a thirty pounder. Though twenty pounders should come along regularly, provided you fish the right waters sensibly, bigger fish really are a law unto themselves. Fish of over twenty-five pounds are rare enough these days for the majority of pike anglers never to have seen one, let alone captured one. Yet luck can see the least experienced angler in the world catch one. What the pike angler seeks to obtain is a control over all the variables which might prevent him catching a big pike. After that a variable amount of luck is required to complete the recipe for success. Fishing for pike is, by its very nature, fairly unselective; a small pike can manage to eat the same sized bait as would be deemed attractive to a 'lunker'. It certainly does not warrant the term specimen hunting. The pike angler's approach is nearly always to catch as many pike as possible. By catching the little ones, the big ones will look after themselves. Seldom in pike fishing does one come across a 'big pike only' water, therefore enjoy them all, for every small pike is still a fish caught and anyway the periods between big fish would be a hell of a bore without them!

Guess the weight! The top fish is in fact heavier than the lower, being 22.09 and 21.02 respectively. The top fish measured 40 inches while the lower was 41½ inches. Pike vary tremendously in shape even in the same water.

21 lb 2 oz.
22 lb 9 oz.

3 Basics

a) PIKE TACKLE

The most difficult (and often least interesting!) chapter of a book is to my mind the one describing the tackle required to fish for the desired species. My fishing tackle is as close to a total shambles as you can get, without affecting its pike-catching performance. This inverted snobbery is certainly not necessary, it is unfortunately a by-product of going fishing too often. While the tackle I use is nowhere near as decrepit as that used by Ray Webb (bless him for giving me someone to look down on!) it would certainly fail to impress many pike anglers, particularly those from down south. In this chapter I intend to draw on Trevor

RODS

Never before has the pike angler been offered such a bewildering choice of rods. Many manufacturers produce their own blanks, while some tackle dealers such as Terry Eustace have their own range of blanks and rods built to their own specification. As far as I am concerned, the choice of fibre glass pike rods and blanks can be made easier by coming to terms with the fact that there are only a handful of different pike fishing tasks which a rod will be required to perform; therefore the range of rods required is very limited. I will mention the rods I use, but the reader must realise that there are many other manufacturers' rods which are just as good. I tend to opt for the best value for money, rather than the brand name. Though there is little doubt that the pleasure of pike fishing can be increased by having a large range of rods, it is not obligatory and most pike anglers could probably manage with just two different types of rod.

As far as the terminology of rod design is concerned I will use the popular term of test curve to denote the power of the rod. This is the amount of force in pounds which is required to pull the rod round so that the tip is at 90 degrees to the butt. Fast taper rods obviously have fine diameter tips and rapidly increase in diameter towards the butt, while slow taper rods will usually be thicker at the tip, the diameter increasing slowly towards the butt. Fast taper rods give rise to a tip action, while slow taper rods sometimes bend all the way down to the butt. It is rather confusing, and misleading to compare test curves of fast taper and slow taper rods. Fast taper rods always seem to me to be much more powerful rods than slow taper ones when you are waving them about, perhaps because of their stiffness. In use they may also seem more powerful when compared with a slow taper rod of a similar test curve. In practice, when it comes to fishing with them, the relative differences in the 'feel' of the rod probably have much more bearing on how the rods perform rather than the apparent power. I select my rods on the basis of horses for courses. Certain types of rod are good all-rounders, while some are more specialised. At the bottom of the range so to speak are the fun rods, which are unspecialised, but nice to use. These include the various derivations of the Richard Walker Mark IV and also some of the lighter blanks available today, including the North Western SS5 which I use regularly. Most of the Mark IV's are 10 feet long while the SS5 is 11 feet. These rods are very much slow taper rods with a lovely through action. They are the ideal rods for fishing small to medium live and deadbaits, provided long distance casting is not required. Because they are through action they will cast fragile baits without snatching them off. They can also be used to give a pike stick, for they are very powerful rods, provided you are not afraid to see them bent double! The carp rods are generally around 1½lb test curve while the SS5 is rated at 2lb. If you are casting baits of less than 6 ounces no further than 60 yards, such rods are all you need. They are ideal for boat fishing and it was the SS5 that landed my biggest pike to date from a boat, 32lb 2oz. Such rods are also ideal for lure fishing with the smaller plugs and spoons. 10 foot rods are adequate for most situations, but where long paternoster tails are used or when fishing in restricted swims with, for instance, reed beds or high banks behind the angler, the extra length of an 11 foot rod is invaluable.

When it comes to fishing big waters, or the bait size is stepped up, more powerful rods are required. Big waters frequently require long distance casting and, because of this, larger baits or heavy leads. I use three different rods for big waters or larger baits. For all my livebaiting with baits up to 10 ounces and long distance casting with 6 to 8 ounce deadbaits, I use an 11 foot slow taper 2¾lb test curve rod. The make is immaterial as many manufacturers supply such blanks. My own is an Oliver's blank, which Terry Eustace described as being suitable for growing beans up! The blank is admittedly rather old-fashioned, being very thick walled and rather heavy. Perhaps one of Terry's 2¾lb pike rods would be preferable, but until it breaks I cannot see any reason to change. Because it is so thick walled it is nearly indestructable, something I value, for thin walled rods do not last long when rolled up with rod rests and other rods in a roll-up holdall. The versatility of my rod is

Mick Cooper plays a Loch Awe pike (*photo Pete Melbourne*).

impressive, for it will cast large livebaits 40 yards without any risk of casting them off, while half mackerel baits are propelled 80 yards with a back or side wind. It is also a very good hooker (excuse the expression!) and a pleasure to play a pike on. It is not a good rod for casting deadbaits into a head wind or for use with small baits and big leads. For small baits and big leads of up to 3 ounces you need a fast taper rod of similar length and test curve. Such rods are numerous and I will only mention the North Western SS6 and PK 3 here, though I have some other rods which do the same job. The fast tip action gets a big lead moving fast and it is the speed of the lead which dictates how far the bait will be thrown (with a backwind a high cast also adds distance). For hurling half mackerel baits into a strong headwind a really meaty rod helps, coupled with a low

In the net, 26 pounds.

trajectory cast. I bought a couple of such rods from Trevor Moss when he switched to carbon rods. They are powerful, almost 'evil' rods and I have no idea what make they are. All I know is that they are very stiff compared with any others in my kit. These rods are invaluable for fishing big pits and loughs from the bank. In these situations the amount of rubbish and boulders on the bed prevents fishing with a lot of lead on the line and casting weight exists solely in the bait. Because of this a full blooded cast is required to overcome, or at least compensate for, the air resistance of a large deadbait. As far as I have noticed there is little difference in the rate of hook pullouts when using very stiff rods compared with soft ones. Provided one anticipates the actions of a pike it is up to the angler to judge the amount of pressure which should be applied or released. It is poor angling that results in lost fish, not the rods! This is a different situation from that experienced by other anglers, particularly those after carp, but then the hook hold in a carp's mouth is rather different from that obtained in a pike!

For heavier lure fishing or deadbait wobbling a stiffer rod such as those just described will be useful. Firstly, because of the weights being cast, and secondly because pike probably hook themselves more effectively when hitting a lure which is attached to a stiff rather than a soft rod. The reverse is the case when trolling deadbaits, for the pike should be able to grab the bait with as little rod top resistance as possible. This allows the angler to give line, allowing time for the pike to get the bait well into its mouth before hitting it. I use my SS5 for deadbait trolling and find it to be ideal. A 21¾lb Irish pike would probably disagree!

For those making their own rods I'll just describe the fittings I have found to be ideal. All my rods are fitted with Fuji or Seymo type rings. I used to have to replace hard chrome rings regularly, due to wear at the solder joins. Since I went over to lined rings I have not replaced a ring in 5 years, neither have I broken any! I reckon the firms that make these rings will go bust before long, due to their immortal nature. Reel fittings are all Fuji clips, mounted direct to the rod handle over a shrink tube sleeve. For thin handles I wind string round to build them up and then slide on the shrink tube; no butt caps or bits and pieces. All rings are whipped on with 15lb Sylcast and no varnish is used. Seems crude I know, but I am more interested in using the rod than looking at it! About a foot from the rod butt I usually tape a piece of curtain wire. This prevents the rod sliding out of rod rests, particularly boat rod rests. These days I seldom make my own rods, having bought some of my mates' rods secondhand. Saves a little work and of course it is cheap as well. Fibre glass rods are near enough indestructible and the need to replace them seldom arises, unless you decide to go up-market and use carbon rods.

Until very recently I had not used a carbon fibre rod of any description. As always the desire to hold on to my money prevented me from going out and buying one. Instead Trevor Moss took pity on me and gave me one of his 11ft, 2lb test curve rods to try. Having used it for most of the season, and 7 twenty pounders having fallen to this rod alone, I think that I can make a fair evaluation. The fact that the rod was made of carbon fibre rather than glass did not influence whether or not I caught those pike. In the situations I found myself in, casting or hooking pike at long distances was not involved.

Despite this I enjoyed using my carbon fibre rod. Because the rod is lighter and more responsive, the feel of the fish is much better. The rod becomes much more of an extension of the arm. Compared with similar test curve glass rods, a carbon rod seems firm and smooth, while a glass rod seems sloppy. So if you have yet to choose your pike rods and can afford to pay a little more, I would advise a carbon fibre rod. If you already have all the gear, I cannot recommend that you get rid of all your glass rods in favour of carbon. However, in the long term, for greater enjoyment it might be worth moving over to carbon rods as the glass rods expire, get trodden or or stolen!

The price of carbon fibre rods is likely to continue to fall and some tackle dealers are talking in terms of switching to carbon only and not bothering to stock glass rods. If the prices do become very close I would agree that glass rods will be a thing of the past. Many anglers are worried about the supposed fragility of carbon rods. Touch wood, I have yet to break one, in spite of doing things you shouldn't do with a relatively light rod, such as punching out half a mackerel into a strong headwind, trolling with rather large deadbaits and, worst of all, chucking the gear in the back of the car in disgust after another blank on the Broads!

At present I am trying out a range of realistically priced carbon pike rods to be marketed by Andy Barker. So far they appear very promising and likely to go down well, at a sensible price.

REELS

Reels are much more important to the pike angler than rods, or should I say the choice of reels. The ideal reel should have a deep wide spool, be designed so as to never get line behind the spool, be fairly free running, but not so much so that it unwinds line all over the place, have a fast rate of line retrieve, have a large knob on the handle so frozen fingers can hold it, be as small as possible, but be able to take 150 yards of 15lb line, and have an efficient slipping cluth, preferably mounted on the rear of the reel.

Looking at the three reels I most often use I find that none are perfect! The Mitchell 410 perhaps comes closest, though the Abu 54 and 55 Cardinal models have some plus points compared with the Mitchell. Unfortunately the Abu has some disadvantages, particularly the price! The choice is very much up to the angler, though I prefer the Mitchells for winter work, due to the large knob on the handle, compared with the hopeless effort on the Abu. For trolling I prefer the Abu reels with stern drags. This is a much less fiddly position for the clutch control. There are other reels and I am sure that some of them are very good indeed. Unfortunately when I asked to have samples for review, no-one bothered to send me them, so the reader will have to try them for himself. As far as other types of reels are concerned, I have never felt the need to buy them, though I have fished with multipliers and centre pins. Multipliers have their exponents, though I myself cannot see the point of using them. I have not felt deprived by not using multipliers, in fact because I use the same fixed spool reels for all my fishing, I am in the fortunate position of knowing my tackle really well. This allows a certain amount of nonchalance, even when playing very big fish. There is never the need to think where the clutch is on this reel, or how much line does it hold!

LANDING NETS

For years I have used a 24 inch round net with a deep knotless net and a 6 foot handle. I have landed a lot of 44 inch pike with no bother at all and do not anticipate any problems with any bigger fish, should I be so lucky. I do own a triangular net, one of Trevor Moss's, a medium sized one with 36 inch arms. Despite this, one thirty pounder went in easily enough. I like this net because the arms are easily tensioned. A Y-shaped alloy moulding is used for the insertion of the solid fibre glass arms, which are held in place by means of the tension cord. This net can be erected and put away in seconds which makes it the ideal boat landing net. The only problem with triangular nets is the tension cord between the arms. A big pike will tend to deform the arms allowing the cord to drop and one which is not really in the net can easily slide out. If the hooks catch in the net the pike can easily be lost, something I found out **in February 1982 when a 20 pound pike made a quick get-away! So with** triangular nets with a tension cord it is essential to get the pike well into the net before lifting. I had a terrible cold when I made my mistake otherwise I would never have panicked and tried to net the fish too soon. All other types of nets are either too heavy or take too long to set up.

KEEP NETS AND SACKS

I have only ever used keep nets to retain pike while I get the camera ready. With the advent of industrial nylon carp sacks made by people like Del Romang, Kevin Nash and Andy Barker, the keep net goes into the dustbin. Even if I have a nylon sack with me I still prefer to release my pike immediately after capture. However if you are stuck for a camera or a witness, a nylon sack (with lots of small holes punched in it) is the answer. Don't put two fish in one sack because they tend to bash each other about when you take them out of the water. I dislike sacking pike mainly because they are too lively when you get them on the bank. Handling a fresh pike is bad for the nerves and the pike.

WEIGHING SLINGS

Though in the past I have weighed pike directly by hooking the scales under the chin, there is a degree of risk with the method, and I have been lucky not to have damaged pike in this manner. Therefore I have moved over to using a weighing sling. This move has been

Two types of landing net, both ideal for landing big pike. On the left the Trevor Moss tensioned arm net, with 36 inch arms, on the right a 24 inch circular net. Both nets have landed pike of 44 inches with ease.

prompted by the production of some efficient slings by people such as Trevor Moss and Andy Barker. Make sure you obtain a sling which is suitable for long fish such as pike. Most pike slings work for carp, but the situation does not always apply in reverse, so if you intend fishing for carp and pike, get a multipurpose one.

FOR GETTING THE TACKLE TO THE WATER!

All my rods are carried ready made up in a roll-up rod holdall as described by Barrie Rickards in 'Fishing for Big Pike'. Spools are tucked into the bottom pockets (push button spools are a boon). The holdall also carries a landing net and handle, rod rests and an umbrella. All the rest of the gear is carried in a framed rucksack obtained from army surplus stores for £6. In the rucksack is carried all the reels, boxes with hooks, leads, floats and bits and bobs. My Avon scales nestle amongst a thick pad of foam rubber in an ice cream container. Cameras and binoculars (bailiff spotting!) also go in, along with unbreakable flasks of stainless steel, which will save you a fortune in the long run, food and deadbaits. Add to this lot lures, buzzers and emergency bait catching gear and you can see that we are equipped for almost any eventuality. The only other addition is a small folding chair. With this lot and a can of livebait a mile walk is not impossible.

Delkim carp sack, for keeping pike while getting the camera set up.

GETTING TO THE WATER

Over the years I have used bikes, mopeds, three wheelers and cars to get to the water along with trains, buses and walking. The keen pike angler would do well to buy a van. Vans cost less to buy, are not so easily spoiled by dirty tackle and livebait cans, and are big enough to sleep in when required. Mine is a Bedford Chevanne, the same as the Chevette. I've done 75,000 miles in it and it has yet to let me down with major trouble. It is fairly comfortable, quiet and reasonable on petrol. It has a lift-up tail gate for putting clothes on in the rain and because it has a low sill can be used as a fishing base on those waters where you can take the car near to the swim. I have a tow bar on mine for the boat.

SURVIVING ONCE YOU GET THERE

Standard equipment includes thermal underwear, sea socks, heavy Arran jumper (hand-knitted by the wife), quilted jacket, and a Thwaites Berwick waxed cotton jacket, good value for money and waterproof. I do not have one of those green fishing suits, but find a standard set of overalls good at keeping jeans clean. Hats, sunglasses and gloves are all very useful, especially those combination mittens and fingerless gloves (again hand-knitted, this time by the wife's sister — get 'em well trained I say!). Snow boots are essential and I favour the Skee-Tex boots. These last well and keep your feet warm. Thigh and chest waders complete the survival kit. For boat fishing leggings and a blanket can also be useful.

SUNDRIES

Over the years I have probably tried all the items available to pike anglers. Obviously during this time I have come down in favour of certain items and although there may be a number of alternative products, there is little point in mentioning all of them, simply because I do not use them. Line is the most vital item of tackle of them all. You can land big pike on the very worst rods and the poorer reels, but you have no chance at all if the line is substandard. For all my English pike fishing I use 11 pound Sylcast which, until recently has, I think, been underrated as far as breaking strain is concerned. Recently the line has been re-rated and now has a more realistic breaking strain. The old 11 pound actually broke at 15 pounds! This season I will be using the new re-rated 11 pound which was previously rated at 9 pound, in situations which demand extra casting distance. Otherwise I will stick with the 11/15lb. which is so strong that accidental breakages are nearly impossible. For my Irish and Scottish fishing I will continue to use Sylcast in 15 pounds, though its actual breaking strain is about 18 pounds. The strong line is not needed to enable the angler to tame the pike, but rather to cope with

The writer's van, a Bedford Chevanne. Drives like a car with the luxury of being able to chuck things in the back regardless. It will also sleep 6 or 7 Trevor Moss's!

abrasion on rocks and sunken trees. I prefer to use line which may seem on the heavy side for most pike fishing simply because one does not have to be quite so fastidious over line care and the extra strength does allow a margin for small nicks and abrasions to the line. Strong lines and playing a pike fairly quickly to the bank is also likely to avoid total exhaustion of the pike. Trace wire is another important item. I use either Marlin Steel (18lb) or Pike Strand (18lb) marketed by Trevor Moss. Both are bronze in colour and provided they are twisted up correctly make first class traces. A new green 15 pound wire trace has also just been made available by Trevor Moss and it is finer and more kink resistant than any of its predecessors. I have used all the other wires available and would not recommend them as highly as the three above, though some anglers get along fine with the various forms of braided Alasticum. Swivels should be good quality — both Abu and Berkley manufacture reliable swivels of the link and plain variety. Hooks are, in many ways, a personal choice. I use all sorts of treble hooks, but would recommend the Partridge outbends and the Stiletto extra strong trebles. Sizes 6 to 10 are the only ones I use with more 8's than any other size in my tackle box. As far as singles are concerned, when I do use them I invariably use some of my larger carp hooks, Au Lion d'Or size 1's. A while ago I bought a load

The complete pike angler. Ben Moore with everything you need times 2. This person was once mistaken for Ray Webb!

of reject Ryder hooks for about 2p each and gave them a try and found that they worked very well indeed. Provided hooks do not snap or straighten, there is little criticism from me. Most are fairly sharp and require testing, touching up and having the barbs squashed before use. There are semi-barbless hooks available with only one barb per treble; however, though perfectly all right for pike fishing, I prefer to de-barb my own hooks. When buying treble hooks always beware of the really soft wired hooks. I do not know who makes them, but it is possible to buy some very poor hooks. It pays therefore to buy brand name hooks from the specialist dealers rather than some trebles from 'Honest Dick's Tackle Shop', out of a tray of assorted hooks!

All leads are best made yourself using moulds, easily obtained by mail order or from your tackle shop. Mine are $\frac{1}{2}$, $\frac{3}{4}$, 1 and 3 ounce sizes, which usually sees me buying the odd in-between size from time to time. No swivels are required in the top of the lead, as copper wire is perfectly adequate. I am thinking at the moment of using other materials for weights, particularly now it has been shown conclusively that lead weights and shot kills swans. I will probably try various numbers of steel nuts as paternoster leads, as these are the ones most frequently lost by the pike angler. One item which will be difficult to replace will be swan shot (not very well named at this point in time). These I tend to use a lot, mainly when adding weight to float legered baits. Being able to pinch them on and take them off easily will be a difficult property to find a substitute for. I also use strips of sheet lead to get baits down when trolling. Cut into a half moon they work very well as anti-kink leads, taking out the twist caused by even the most gently revolving bait.

Floats need only a short mention as my selection is fairly basic in nature. For sunken paternoster work I use one inch pilot floats, preferably painted a drab colour such as olive green or brown. For surface fishing I use $1\frac{1}{4}$ and $1\frac{1}{2}$ inch pilot floats. If you can get them (I believe that tackle dealers will soon be stocking them) $1\frac{1}{2}$ inch polystyrene balls make ideal floats, the hole through the middle being made with a hot screwdriver. I have used some of these since I nicked them from chemistry lessons in 1970! They are easily painted, but beware of using any paint which contains acetone as a solvent: they melt. Fluorescent red can be painted on directly without a white undercoat and because of this they also make ideal bobbins for legering. For jobs which require greater visibility of the float, end ring sliders are essential. These are very easily made out of round section balsa wood, with or without a dowel stem. Several different sizes are carried and these can be changed rapidly using a link swivel. I seldom use vaned floats, preferring to

The writer's pike kit of 1973, little changed today. The dead roach is an optional extra! These days traces are wound round a foam rubber 'Swiss roll' and kept in one of the plastic boxes shown. Livebait snatching gear is kept in the van, rather than carried down the bank.

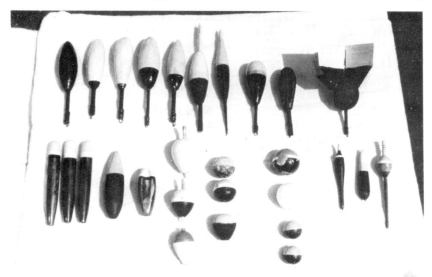

A selection of pike floats, including end ring sliders (top row) and various sliders and pike bungs proper. The floats fourth from the right (bottom row) are used most by the author and are either 1½ inch polystyrene balls or 1½, 1¼ and 1 inch pilot floats.

balloon baits out, but there is a good case for having a vaned float in your tackle box, particularly if the balloons are running short! Vaned floats must be self-cocking, so they must carry enough lead wire to make them stand up. Vanes are simply pieces of X-ray film fitted at right angles into two slots in the top of the float. Many shop-bought floats have large holes through them. I solve this problem by glueing electrical wire sleeving into the hole. This reduces the diameter and prevents the float slipping down over the link swivel attached to the wire trace. Plastic beads from cheap Woollies necklaces are used in various situations, but mainly between float and stop knots.

Bite indication when legering requires some thought. Rod rests can be dispensed with for float fishing, but when legering you cannot do without them. I use a variety of rod rests, some of them found on the bank. Someone, somewhere has probably got some of my rod rests! Extending rests are almost essential and the better quality ones are preferable. Trevor Moss does a good range and the ultimate rod rests are the Elite range made by Dellareed, the manufacturers of the Optonic bite indicator. Tops are numerous and include home-made efforts. In specialised situations buzzer bars, tripods and the like can come in handy and the above people supply all these items.

Close up of simple bobbin. Mervyn Wilkinson gave me this one in 1977. A run either pulls the line out of the clip or it drops back.

MM1 indicator. In position for run detection.

MM1 in action. Bleep tone inside tells you when you're *in*.

Two rod leger set-up with bobbins.

As far as bite indicators are concerned, the ordinary Optonics, the type with a remote sounder box are quite usable in a pike fishing situation, though they can be annoying when the weather is windy ('bleep, bleep, bleep'). I use mine on a Dellareed buzzer bar and tape the sounder box onto the bar. Some day I'll put Terry clips on the box. This works well and in conjunction with a bobbin gives good indication of all types of run and also registers the amount of bait activity when sunken paternostering. The various types of indicators which use bobbins and arms are ideal for the pike angler as they register drop backs as well as conventional runs. I have used Trevor Moss's MM1 for a full season and can recommend it. It uses a Mercury tilt switch inside the casing, which allows different bobbins with different tensions to be employed. Several other indicators are available, but unfortunately I have not used them myself. However, talking to people who have, suggests that these work very well. These include indicators made by Andy Barker, Jack Simpson (Eddy Turner design) and Gardner Tackle. I have a copy of an Eddy Turner indicator, which uses a microswitch and cam rather than a Mercury tilt switch. It works well enough and costs very little to make.

For all my buzzerless legering or sunken paternostering I use table tennis balls or polystyrene ball bobbins. These have wire clips in one end and are attached by cord to the rod using a crocodile clip. Gardner tackle have come up with some adjustable run clips which have, as far as I am concerned, superseded the old form of sprung metal clip.

As far as sundries are concerned there are only a few minor items which may prove useful. Baiting needles, candle wax for spigot ferrules, line floatant, spare rod rings, sharp scissors, bait cutting knife, hook sharpening stone and pen to make notes with, about complete the sundries. Rubber bands or run clips for holding the line to the rod butt are required and a selection is carried either in the tackle box or in position on the rods. All these items are carried in either a large Stewart box or a variety of ice cream containers. One final item deserves particular attention, and that is weighing scales. There is little point weighing a fish if the weight is going to be in error. I have mine regularly 'weights and measure' tested and I'm pleased to say that they continue to tell the truth. The onus is on the angler to make sure his scales weigh correctly. I do not believe in adding or subtracting weight after the event. It weighs what it weighs and if your scales are wrong, hard luck! I use Avon Dial scales, which at a pinch can cope up to 33 pounds (by zeroing on minus weights). I intend to get a set of Salter tubular scales for fish up to 44 pounds. I always carry a tape measure with the scales as length statistics can be interesting. Remember to measure the pike from tip of the nose to fork of the tail, without following the contour of the body. Following the body and not keeping the tape straight can add several inches!

b) PUTTING THE TACKLE TOGETHER AND USING IT!

As in previous chapters I will describe *my* approach to the subject, in this case making up terminal tackles, casting, striking and playing pike. Other pike anglers will have different ways of doing certain things and they may, as a result, fish just as efficiently as myself. However I will restrict myself to how I approach things and I feel that if it good enough for a fairly incompetent angler such as myself, it should be OK for the rest of the pike angling world!

Simplicity is an important consideration and I can see no point in complicating what is in essence a very easy and simple way of fishing. Terminal tackles should be as simple as possible and the minimum number of hooks used. All my pike traces are usually 18 to 24 inches

ATTACHING TRACE WIRE TO SWIVEL OR HOOK

1. PASS LOOP OF WIRE THROUGH EYE OF SWIVEL OR TREBLE AND PASS OVER TREBLE OR SWIVEL.

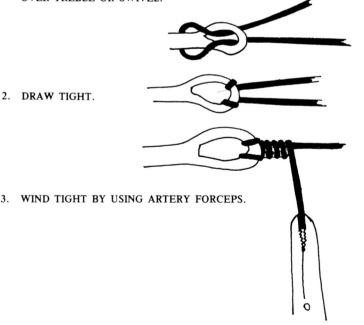

2. DRAW TIGHT.

3. WIND TIGHT BY USING ARTERY FORCEPS.

BASIC PIKE TRACES

1. STANDARD TANDEM TREBLE RIG. SOMETIMES KNOWN AS SNAP TACKLE
    WHEN USING THE TRADITIONAL 'JARDINE' TREBLES. BOTH TREBLES
    ARE FIXED IN POSITION AND THE SPACING IS SELECTED ACCORDING TO
    BAIT SIZE. SEE INSET FOR METHOD OF HOLDING SECOND TREBLE IN
    POSITION.

2. SINGLE AND A TREBLE — FOR WHEN A BAIT DOES NOT DEMAND TWO
    TREBLES, BUT MORE THAN JUST A SINGLE TREBLE. ALSO FOR WHEN
    ADDITIONAL HOOKHOLD IS REQUIRED, I.E. FOR SOFT BAITS SUCH AS
    SARDINES.

3. SINGLE TREBLE.

4. SINGLE HOOK.

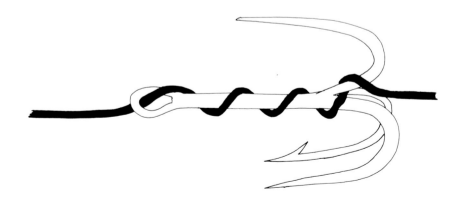

long and consist of the hooks and wire and nothing else. Traces (except those used for spinning or deadbait wobbling) do not need a swivel at the line end. Instead I make a simple loop which is attached to the line by means of a link swivel. This approach has many advantages; foremost is the fact that the trace can be removed without having to re-tie knots. Where very difficult swims are being fished, the trace can be unclipped and you can struggle up the bank with just the pike in the net and no rod to carry. The lack of a swivel on the trace also allows the bait to be threaded easily through the tail root. All my traces are made from either Marlin Steel or Pikestrand and the new green 15lb Pikestrand marketed by Trevor Moss is probably the best wire available. It does not fray, can be twisted with fingers and twists up very neatly with forceps. To make a trace take a 24 inch piece of wire; make a loop at one end and hold loop and wire, attaching forceps to loose end. Simply whirl forceps round until twisted and cut off the short piece remaining. At the business end, slide the second treble up the trace and make a loop at the other end. Pass the loop through the eye of the treble, pass over treble and pull tight. Twist up as before. Traces are kept in a plastic box, wound around a foam 'swiss roll'. This will carry eight or nine, ample for a day's

LONG RANGE LEGER

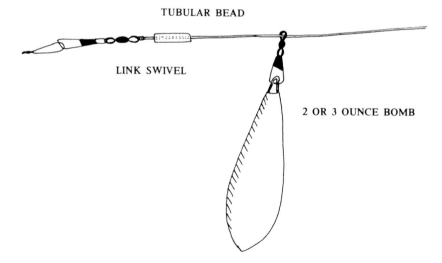

TUBULAR BEAD

LINK SWIVEL

2 OR 3 OUNCE BOMB

TO HELP AVOID TANGLES IT PAYS TO USE A LONG 24 INCH WIRE TRACE.

fishing. As far as line knots are concerned I use the standard tucked blood knot and always test the knot before use. I also always test the first couple of yards of line and the trace before use and after every fish. This extra care has resulted in a remarkable decrease in the number of break-offs due to damaged lines and traces.

When legering I often use a bead between the link swivel and the lead, to prevent the lead locking on the knot. When using big leads up to 3 ounces I use a long tubular bead as obtained from certain types of cheap necklace. This encourages the lead to separate slightly from the trace on the cast. Provided you close the bale arm and tighten up as the lead and bait drops through the water, tangles are avoided.

Stop knots for float fishing are the standard Billy Lane stop knot, tied with a 8 to 10lb line and whenever you move it wet the line to prevent friction damaging the line. When using end ring slider floats which are attached using a link swivel, it is easy to switch to legering; simply remove the stop knot and substitute a lead for the float. It is this type of simple versatility which makes fishing less of a chore and slightly more effective.

BILLY LANE SLIDING FLOAT STOP KNOT

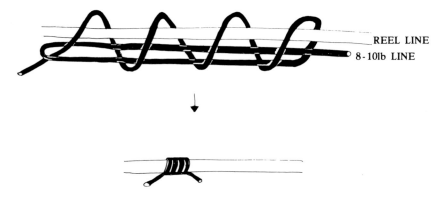

REEL LINE
8-10lb LINE

The actual job of casting baits out may seem rather obvious, however to get the best out of your tackle does take some practice. When casting livebaits and soft deadbaits with slow action rods, we are aiming to get the bait out as far as possible without casting the bait off. To do this we use the action of the rod to accelerate the bait gently before releasing the line. A soft rod can be used with considerable force to cast a bait out, usually casting high to use a back-wind or keeping the cast low in a head wind. For longer distance casting with larger baits which do not fly off the hooks, the aim is to push forward with one arm and push down on the rod butt with the other. The rod is bent considerably and the bait is projected at some speed out to the desired spot. With big leads, small baits and fast taper rods, casting becomes akin to beach fishing! For ultimate distance with big leads a shock leader can be used to enable more force to be used, meanwhile using a lighter reel line. The shock leader should be around 18lb b.s. while reel line should not go below 8lb b.s. When casting, at least a yard of the shock leader should be wound onto the reel.

It is not often that you have to be spot on when casting pike baits, but it pays to develop the ability, for there are times when you can drop a bait on top of a striking pike and catch it. For total accuracy an overhead cast takes some beating. In fact if you watch any of the better swim feeder anglers in action, you will notice that they favour the overhead cast. Also being able to drop a bait in the right place first time saves bait and avoids the bloke next door (usually Bryan Culley!) walking over to sort you out. In strong winds you must obviously compensate on the cast. Where space is available I usually walk up wind and cast slightly down and across. This increases distance and puts the bait in the right place without too big a bow forming. A large bow of line can easily form and as soon as the bait hits the water it pays to flick the bow over to straighten the line. By winding in a bit of line it is usually possible to arrive at a reasonable degree of contact with the bait.

The runs you get while pike fishing obviously vary from day to day and water to water. I love the sizzling runs you get on Irish and Scottish lochs. When you get to the rod the line is usually melting off the spool. On other waters you frequently get a short run away from you and then the pike starts to come back in. I never strike when the pike is swimming towards me. This is the one big advantage of a float. Provided it is on the surface it enables you to decide which way to strike. To strike when the fish is swimming towards you increases the chance of pulling the hooks out of its mouth, so I either wait until a better opportunity is presented or I move to the right side of the pike. Very few pike fail to give a good indication and provided you are attentive you should be able to see the early stages of a run. Both Dave Moore and I saw the first gentle bobs of my float once while fishing on a calm day and we were about 100 yards apart! The result was a 15lb pike which soon got into its stride and ran off fast.

The actual hooking of the pike can result in some of the most comical antics known to the pike angler. There is absolutely no need to perform one, two or three hard jerking strikes. Pike angling is totally different from most other forms of freshwater fishing. When a pike takes a bait it holds it with its powerful jaws. I doubt if any amount of striking could shift the bait and hooks and it is much more likely that you would move the pike before you moved the bait. In fact this happens with small pike, which frequently clamp onto the bait and because of their small size offer so little resistance that you do not hook them until they shake their heads to get rid of the bait. Then of course they do this at the net and get off! The pike angler aims to maintain a constant pressure on the fish, until it tries to throw the bait. The moment it starts to release its grip on the bait the hooks go in (or should!). With most pike this happens soon after you have tightened to the fish. The essence of the strike, if you could call it that, is a quick wind down to the fish until you can wind no more, then a gentle, but firm, sweep back of the rod. The pressure is then kept on the pike, for any slackening can give it a good chance of getting off. Some pike fight very hard and it is usual to give a lot of line to these pike. I never use a slipping clutch for playing pike; instead I always have the anti reverse off and simply backwind as required. I have never had any trouble backwinding and that includes when fishing for pike, carp, trout and other species capable of running fast. The fast retrieve reels are good for backwinding as it is much easier to keep up with the pike. The only time I use a slipping clutch is when trolling with deadbaits. This allows the pike to take the bait with less resistance.

Provided you stay calm it is almost impossible to lose a pike due to breakages while playing. The most dangerous moments are when a pike tries to take you unaware. Sometimes when you strike the pike accelerates off hard. The rod slams over and if you are daft enough to have the anti-reverse on — crack! Obviously you must anticipate such events and providing you are ready to backwind you will soon be out of trouble. Tail walking pike provide a bit of excitement, but provided you keep the rod down low, again there is no problem. The important thing is to keep the line tight, for a tail walking pike usually shakes its head and hooks can be thrown clear at this point. Loch pike are also particularly prone to going nuts as you get them near to the bank or boat. At all costs a pike should not be allowed to get under the boat; if it does you will have to lift the second anchor (if down) and slack off and allow the pike to swim around while you sort out the mess.

I have never been in this unfortunate position, but I hope that I will not panic when it does happen. All the text book instruction in the world will not get you out of trouble. It is rather like being in a car accident, you only have seconds to respond and several alternatives to choose. By being calm you are perhaps more likely to choose the best alternative.

Though I have made it clear that hooking pike does not demand theatrical actions, there are some situations where unusual tactics can help. At extreme long range I generally walk back as I bend into a pike. This rather severe treatment of the pike tends to maintain a really hard pull on the fish until it is hooked. It all looks rather strange, but can work well enough to make the odd looks worthwhile.

Throughout this chapter I have placed considerable emphasis on simplicity and the reader will notice that I use very few 'brilliant ideas' to enable me to catch pike. This demonstrates my philosophy towards pike fishing, which is being devoted towards understanding the behaviour of the pike and then using fairly basic, but deadly effective, methods to catch them. Other anglers have no doubt shown considerable ingenuity in their pike fishing and every so often such innovators come up with something that is of use to us all. For the most part new ideas and techniques play a very minor role in catching pike.

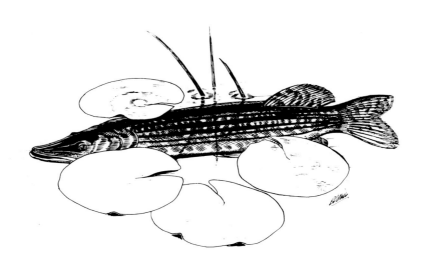

4 Handling, Unhooking & Conservation

If, like me, you enjoy catching plenty of good-sized pike, in good condition, in nice surroundings, then you should be keen on all aspects of pike handling, for there is little doubt that the period a pike spends on the bank is potentially the most dangerous one of its life. With the wrong person in charge the events which lead to the death or damage of the pike are so obvious to the experienced pike angler. The remedy then is to educate the novice angler, firstly not to kill the pike, and secondly to handle the fish with care.

The formation and growth of the Pike Anglers Club, preceded by the Pike Society has, without doubt, resulted in far more big pike being returned alive to the water. The brainchild of Barrie Rickards and Hugh Reynolds has caused a change in attitudes in many parts of the country. The work continues under new management (the old timers needed a rest!) from Norwich with John Watson as secretary. The PAC serves a social function as well as a political role, though many believe that the political role is of the highest priority. Together with bodies such as the National Association of Specialist Anglers, the PAC has placed members on the consultative associations which advise the Water Authorities around the country. In this way the pike angler has a voice where it matters and can influence the policies of the Water Authorities. PAC members are also active at club level, advocating rules which ensure the return of pike and fighting against livebait bans.

Membership of PAC is simply a matter of sending (at the time of writing) £5 to Martyn Page, 10 Britannia Road, Norwich, Norfolk NR1 4HP. PAC members get a well-produced magazine, 'Pikelines', every quarter and regional branches are widespread so that each PAC member can meet other pike anglers at regular meetings. The other body which fights for specimen hunters' rights, often with the PAC, is the NASA, and £5 membership sent to Lyn Culley, 16 Windsor Close, Quorn, Leicestershire, ensures that you have done everything possible to help pike fishing at a national level.

My own views of pike conservation are sometimes at variance with other pike anglers, but on one point I think we are all agreed. That is, that all big pike should be returned alive to the water, and where this is not always possible, on, for instance, trout fisheries, such pike should be transferred elsewhere. By big pike, I refer to fish over 10lbs. In many situations there is also a need to return all pike caught, for pike fisheries are about catching pike of all sizes, not just big ones. From this I think it is clear that I and most other pike anglers are against the killing of big pike for any reason, particularly for mounting as trophies. It always amazes me how a highly respected angler will return a 20lb carp and then the same season kill a big pike to have it mounted. The lack of logic behind this thinking makes me wonder what goes on in some anglers' minds. Though there is little excuse for sending your big pike to the taxidermist, there are mitigating circumstances. Should a big pike die, normally a very rare event and often a by-product of bad handling, then it is perhaps best to have it mounted. A hole in the ground is a far worse fate. Pike anglers who remove big pike from private waters for setting up are perhaps a little different from those who remove fish from public or accessible waters. Their actions are unlikely to affect you or me and it is much more likely that their own sport will suffer as a result. Pike anglers cannot really dictate the behaviour of individuals on private waters, though there is no reason why they cannot try to prevent such actions by talking to the anglers or owners. On public waters the situation is different and every effort should, and usually is, made to prevent big pike from being killed. A good example occurred a couple of years ago when an angler killed a 30 pounder captured from Hollowell Reservoir. The fact that this fish had only recently been saved during the draining off of nearby Ravensthorpe Reservoir made his actions even more regrettable. After that, pressure was brought on the Anglian Water Authority via the consultative committee and a rule protecting all pike over 10lb was imposed. Since then Hollowell has continued to produce good pike to the many anglers who have fished the water.

All over the country the PAC has helped to prevent the killing of big pike and because of this pike fishing is actually improving despite increased pressure from pike anglers. The River Bure in Norfolk is a good example. In the mid seventies local anglers killed a lot of big pike, but today with the vast majority of big pike being returned, the pike fishing is getting better all the time. Even youngsters are learning fast that pike are better returned and that there is no good reason for killing them.

Though things seem to be getting better in certain areas, there is a lot more to do before pike are preserved on a national scale. At the beginning of this chapter I used the term 'Conservation' rather than preservation. This is because conservation in my book refers to management rather than plain preservation of pike at all costs. Pike are just like any other fish and in order to get the best quality pike fishing it may be necessary to manipulate pike stocks. We must not be afraid to do this manipulation even though it may involve the movement, introduction or disposal of pike. Predator and prey should always exist in 'balance'. The term 'balance' is a bit misleading as most fish populations are always changing and the term 'dynamic equilibrium' is perhaps better applied to predator/prey relations. Prey should always be sufficient for the predators to show good growth and also in most waters to provide good fishing for the ordinary angler. Prey shortages may lead to pike going back in condition, showing no growth and eventually dying. In these situations it may be vital to the well-being of the fishery to remove some of the pike, preferably the smaller ones, and either transfer them if possible, or at worst kill them. Such situations are fortunately rare and should be identified with the help of the local Water Authority fisheries unit.

On many waters the pike have been killed in order to promote the interests of the non-predatory fish. This usually results in an explosion of small pike numbers with little benefit to the general fishing. In my work I come across such waters regularly and I advise the clubs or owners to stop killing the pike until a normal population is attained. Some removal of very small pike may be required, but the aim of re-establishing big pike can make this unnecessary.

It is almost always true that good pike waters are also good roach, bream or whatever waters. The reverse is of course also often true! There are many good match waters up and down the country which have a large head of pike; the Severn, Trent and Witham being good examples. The pike do not seem to adversely affect the other fish and why should they? Evolution has resulted in natural control factors, such as cannibalism, poor spawning years, and natural mortality, giving rise to fairly stable predator/prey balances. Our role should be to make compensating changes in fisheries affected by unnatural factors such as pike killing and pollution. Sometimes this will require stocking with big pike and there is some good evidence available to indicate that this can do no harm to the ordinary fishing, yet enhance the pike fishing beyond recognition. One water I used to fish had very few big pike due to pike killing. Things changed eventually and it was then safe to consider a little stocking. About 5 doubles were introduced up to 18 pounds and subsequently the pike fishing became worthwhile. The roach and bream fishing remained as good as ever. Fish kills sometimes result in a need for pike stocking as pike seem more susceptible to deoxygenation in particular. Several waters I fish have been seeded with small to medium-sized pike, fish of 8 to 10 pounds. These waters have now recovered and are producing twenty pounders each winter. It would have taken several more years for this to have come about naturally.

All the care in the world in the managing of waters is worthless if the anglers fishing the waters are unable to return their pike in pristine condition. The two most important things to remember are: unhooking the pike without damage, and, while the pike is on the bank, avoiding injury. I've not mentioned landing pike as most anglers these days use knotless landing nets. Having seen gaff-damaged pike, presumably landed by anglers who thought they were proficient in its use, I would strongly suggest that the best place for a gaff would be as a full-time meat hook in a butcher's. There is only one word of advice I could give to the would-be gaff user and that is — don't.

The old excuse that hooks get tangled up in landing nets is a joke. If the hooks are hanging out of the pike's mouth, you land it by hand; the forefinger being used to lift the pike out under the chin, taking care not to get your hand near the hooks. The biggest pike I have landed doing this weighed 25¼ pounds and this was followed by another twenty the same day, landed in just the same way. If I can do it, so can you! A leather or thick rubber glove can be used as an aid to hand landing, but I prefer no artificial aids.

Once landed, the pike should be removed from the landing net, as they sometimes tangle themselves up in it. Placed on soft grass or anything soft and wet in the bottom of the boat, the pike must be restrained and not allowed to knock itself silly. When a pike's head thumps against even soft ground the resulting thud should tell you that it is just like someone banging your head against the floor. So either lift the pike off the ground with your finger under the chin or sit astride it. Either way if it starts to struggle, something you will soon be able to anticipate as the pike stiffens before moving, hold the fish firmly to your body. Do not drop it or hold it so hard that you remove scales. Once it calms down you can get on with the job of unhooking it.

For unhooking you will need one essential piece of equipment and three optional ones. Essential equipment is a good pair of long artery forceps which lock efficiently. Other bits and pieces, such as a thick glove, long handled wire cutters and heavy duty, thick nosed forceps can be very useful — the glove for protection of the hand while inserting your fingers under the chin, the wire cutter to chop up the one in a thousand very difficult hook and the thick forceps for getting a good grip on the bait's tail, prior to pulling it out of the throat when it has been swallowed. The extra forceps are also handy should you require additional help to clear the hooks of folds of flesh in the pike's throat.

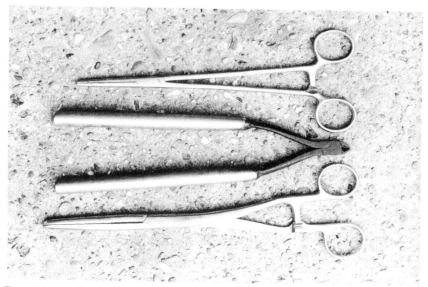

Essential gear. Top, standard long nosed forceps. Middle, home-made long handled wire cutters. Bottom, extra thick nosed forceps.

There should never be any reason to leave hooks in pike, even though the normal bronze treble hooks will dissolve in time with the action of the pike's stomach acids. During the 1981/82 season I caught well over 150 pike and, though a proportion had swallowed the bait further than I would have liked, all hooks were removed and no fish as far as I know suffered from the experience.

Hook removal is facilitated by using barbless or flattened barbed hooks, by using the smallest size of treble practical, and by not using more than two trebles on a bait. Pike hooked in the mouth are easily dealt with, if you remember to ease the hooks out rather than tear them out. To look at some pike you would think that the captor had put his left boot on the pike grabbed the trace and pulled. Deeply seated hooks are no problem provided the following procedure is adopted. Get the pike on the ground with your finger under the chin. With the pike upside down the mouth drops open. If it does not, pull back the lower jaw with the hand which is being used to hold it under the chin, and the tail of the bait should then be visible if it is still there. Then pull it out using the thick nosed forceps. Try and get the bait out whole as tearing the bait is messy and makes the job more difficult. After this, or if no bait is present, firmly pull the trace until the first treble appears. If it does not appear, work the thin nosed forceps in through the most posterior gill arch and reach down the trace until you grip the hook. The hook can then be drawn up in sight, by extending the gut. The gut is quite invertable so do not worry too much about this, but do not pull so hard as to rip the stomach wall. Once in sight turn the treble over so the points are facing away from you, and at least one of the prongs should come away immediately. To free the others, turn through 360 degrees and the next prong should come clear. In dire circumstances, usually brought on by the one bait-holding barb being well imbedded, wire cutters can be used to snip through the bend of the hook. Fortunately having to do this is so rare these days that my wire cutters stand a good chance of going rusty. The second treble frequently comes clear or is easily pulled into view. Repeat the process and that is that! Sounds simple and indeed it is, provided you are confident and careful. With a little experience, best obtained in the company of more experienced pike men, anyone can make a good job of unhooking pike. After doing this to a lot of pike over the years and subsequently recapturing the same fish later (some on the same day!), I have no doubt at all that possibly every single fish survives the experience. Pike after all eat all sorts of spiney finned fish, such as sticklebacks, perch and ruffe, and I suspect that the stomach wall is perforated quite often. Being a self-sealing organ, the stomach can take a lot of punishment. In fact, one day, while fishing on Hollowell Reservoir, I saw caught a fish of about 8lbs with a large single protruding from its underside. This hook had obviously worked its way through the stomach wall and then through the body wall. All this had not put it off feeding, it being very much alive and well!

What does kill pike is leaving big hooks inside them, either by being unable to remove them, or by snapping off. If a large treble or single penetrates the gut wall and works its way upwards into the heart or into the liver, then bleeding is likely to occur, and I do not rate a pike's chances at all highly in this situation. Similarly a blocked gullet caused by very large trebles (I've seen 1/0s in pike throats) can cause starvation. Hooks in the corner of the mouth, thus preventing jaw movement and leading to suffocation can also arise due to break offs. None of these causes of death are likely to arise provided hooks are small and lines and traces are sound.

A new gadget called the 'Deep Throat Pike Disgorger' has proved to be very useful in the removal of deep-seated de-barbed or barbless trebles. It is available from Alan Brown and Trevor Moss.

To pick a pike up simply slip the forefinger under the chin. A thick glove provides useful protection from accidental contact with the teeth!

Sitting astride a big pike with the finger under the chin enables the mouth to be opened. Forceps can then be inserted through the gill arches to enable inverting and removal of any deeply seated hooks.

Pike hooked in the gill rakers bleed a lot, but this may not always be fatal. Indeed on some hard fished waters many pike are swimming around with broken gill rakers caused by poor handling. Though bleeding from the gills appears serious, the blood quickly clots and most fish survive. There is certainly little evidence to advocate putting the pike out of its misery. If you could ask the pike I am sure it would agree to being allowed to take its chances. I have had zander of up to nine pounds bleed all over the place, yet a year later the same tagged fish has been caught again. Zander are generally more fragile than pike so if a zander can survive a massive haemorrhage then a pike must have a good chance. Hooks in gill rakers have to be removed carefully and sometimes it is as well to cut the hook point off rather than risk additional damage.

Once unhooked the whole process of weighing and photography should take only a few minutes. I usually weigh my pike under the chin, taking care to hold the fish if it struggles. The hook of the balance is slid along the bottom edge of the gill cover until it reaches the point where both operculi meet. I find this method quick and trouble-free. Unfortunately there is an element of risk involved and I would therefore suggest that a weighing sling or bag should be used. First wet the bag, shake off excess moisture, then zero the scales. (I use Avon dial scales weighing

While unhooking a pike, it may sometimes be preferable to lift it off the ground. Some control is lost when the fish jumps. This 18 pounder was caught by Dave Phillips.

up to 32 pounds, though you can get a reading up to 33 pounds if you zero at minus eight ounces!) Pop the pike into the bag and weigh. For really heavy fish a friend's help is invaluable or use Steve Harper's idea of using a landing net handle to lean on and use it to steady your hands (they should be shaky if it is that big!). While setting up the scales and camera I usually cover the pike's head with a towel, which helps to keep it quiet. Holding a fish for a photograph should be done in such a way that it cannot jump out of your hands. Really big pike are certainly a handful so always take your photos with you kneeling down — the higher up you are, the further to the ground if it does escape your grasp. I generally put one hand under the head and the other under the underside of the fish, just in front of the anal fin. This shows the fish to advantage and also enables it to be hugged to the body if it struggles. Another popular shot is with the finger of one hand under the chin, the other supporting the underside.

I generally do not retain pike unless light conditions really are bad and the flash is on the blink! The industrial nylon carp sacks as marketed by Del Romang, Andy Barker and Kevin Nash are ideal for retaining a pike for a short while, but only one to a sack, please. This is because, though the pike will be undamaged while in the sack, as you lift them out they are likely to knock hell out of each other! Keepnets of any type of material are for emergency use only and last season I finally scrapped mine, having only used it a couple of times a season. Pike struggle too much in keepnets and soon redden up, so my advice is not to use them. Because of this habit of not retaining pike, until recently I have never had a photo of two twenties in a day, though I have been in this fortunate position several times. However, as luck would have it in February of 1982 I had just landed a 21.02 on one rod when the other rod was away before I could set the camera up. So I sacked the first one quickly and then landed another of 22.09! Hence the picture of two twenties in a day.

I think I have made it fairly clear that pike can survive repeated captures with little mortality provided care is taken. However once in a while something happens which can result in the death of a pike. Popularly known as 'gassing up', this was first mentioned by Terry Eustace in a follow-up to his 'Pike Hunt' series in 'Angling' magazine. He experienced this while catching some very hard fighting pike from Ireland, out of 18 to 20 feet of water. Since then, several other anglers have related similar experiences. The pike generally have come up belly up, after having been returned. Some do not even have the strength to swim off. The cure for this has ranged from anchoring the fish on a buoy, out in deeper water, to expelling air by bending the fish. I have had the same

Members of the Soar Valley Specimen Group watch as a weight of 22 pounds is recorded.

An old friend, this one, the fifth time of capture to my rod. Despite the frequent visits to the bank, this is still a very nice fish to look at. Weight 21.13½.

problems myself, once with a gravel pit fish of 18½lb, the other time with a 20.06 from Ireland. Until I caught the 20 which turned up on its belly after return in spite of being caught in only four feet of water, I thought it was a 'bends' effect caused by rising too fast out of deep water. I now know that this is not the case. Pike have a duct connecting the swim bladder with the gullet, thus allowing adjustment of air volume in the swim bladder, so distension of the swim bladder, or gassing up, is not really the problem. Neither do I accept the likelihood of the bends; far too many pike survive very rapid depth changes for nitrogen bubbles in the bloodstream to have a serious effect. What does cause pike to turn up is exhaustion. Both my 'belly up' pike fought like stink and almost certainly built up a large oxygen debit. (This is when an animal does so much exercise that the muscles are no longer able to obtain enough oxygen.) This debit results in an accumulation of lactic acid which can later be broken down while the animal is at rest, as the oxygen supply catches up with demand. 'Belly up' pike are I believe suffering from lactic acid accumulation and need time to recover. This recovery period should be with the fish upright (fish on their backs do not seem to rest properly or recover quickly) and in clean oxygenated water. I have had success in recovering my two problem fish, by sitting them upright in a

Getting the length of a 24 pound Irish pike. Note that Andy Barker has the tape following the contour of the body. For a correct length it would be better to lay the pike on the tape.

foot of water, propped up by unlikely things such as bank sticks and rod rests. The 18½ pound fish took eight hours to recover, but was caught two years later 5 pounds bigger. The Irish fish crashed out of my make-shift recovery cradle in no uncertain manner. I hate to say this, but I feel that any other methods of trying to save pike are unlikely to work, in spite of the thought behind them. A fit healthy pike can swim off and get back down to a depth where the pressure on the swim bladder returns to normal, with no difficulty. The only reason pike belly up is because they are exhausted, not because of there being too much air in the swim bladder. Attempting to expel this will not help a pike recover, only rest will do this. The more a pike is messed about the more likely it is to die.

So far in my pike fishing life I have yet to have a double figure pike die on me, though one fish which banged its head rather hard due to my carelessness, might not have made it a few years ago. The odd small fish have died, but these are generally more difficult to unhook due to the confined space you have to work in. The simple rules of pike handling should enable any angler to return his pike alive. I am not impressed by anglers who claim their pike died on them.

Hundreds of photographs and a night in your bath are both good ways of ending up with a corpse. Strike early whenever possible, there being no excuse for waiting if you are incompetent at unhooking. A slightly more relaxed approach is all right provided you have been taught how to unhook your pike properly. Never stand by and watch another angler struggling to unhook a pike, offer help and it will usually be accepted. Never stand by and let another angler kill a big pike. Challenge him in as nice a way as possible and whenever possible use club rules or water authority byelaws (such as they are) to avoid pike killing. Never get involved in heavy aggro, though a show of force behind a particularly ignorant pike angler can help! Most important of all remember that it is your pike fishing you are trying to conserve and to do this you must be up to scratch as a pike angler.

5 Livebaiting

Few subjects create greater rifts between pike anglers than live-baiting. Some say it is essential, others that it is unnecessary. The one fact which escapes most people who get involved in these arguments is that the pike's natural food is invariably live fish. Pike of course also find dead fish quite naturally, but I think it would be safe to say that live fish are more numerous in our fisheries than dead ones and that pike have to capture live fish to meet most of their food requirement. If this were not the case pike could surely have evolved without the streamlining and grouping of the dorsal and anal fin near the tail. Instead of a mouth filled with teeth all that would be required would be a shovel-like gap at one end!

Livebaiting is not a particularly sociable act. Anything which demands the insertion of hooks into live fish and casting with some force out into the water can hardly *not* be classed as cruel. However without going into a lot of argument about other aspects of life being cruel it is difficult to defend the method. In fact some pike anglers no longer use the method due to the cruelty aspect. The only justification I will offer for using this method is that it catches pike and that in some waters it is almost essential to livebait. Having accepted this, I can then go pike fishing knowing that I will deadbait or use an alternative method whenever possible, but will livebait when I feel I have to. It is the freedom to choose which I feel is so essential. Every angler has a conscience and it is up to him to use it rather than having someone else's conscience forced on him. Without this freedom, angling will soon be a thing of the past.

Those who choose to livebait do not do so without considerable effort and risks to themselves. Catching and keeping livebaits is a constant struggle and the law of the land most definitely frowns on the moving of bait fish from one area to another. As a Fishery Inspector for a Water Authority myself, I face the dilemma of having to enforce the law and the law says that live fish must not be transferred from one water to another. Actually catching someone in the act and proving it in court is another thing, so this particular law is difficult to enforce and pike anglers generally disregard it. It would be much easier to comply with the law if livebaiting was allowed provided the water from where the livebait were obtained was connected or close to the water being fished.

After all, fish can travel long distances through river and canal systems spreading diseases if they wish, so why then can the pike angler not do the same thing? Catch the bait from the River Grot to use in the nearby and connected Septic drain! Another system which could be developed is the screening of certain waters or river systems and issuing of health certifications or restrictions as the case may be. Pike anglers could then catch bait from such cleared waters and take them to waters of their choice. Unfortunately all this is probably too much trouble for the authorities concerned and it is more likely that livebaiting will be banned. Then the exponents of the method will simply go 'underground' and any possible control of the method will be lost.

For the purposes of the rest of this section it has to be assumed that some bending of the rules is inevitable. I am neither endorsing such rule bending or encouraging it; I am simply describing it. It is up to the individual whether or not he is prepared to take the risks involved. The biggest and most tedious problem facing the pike angler is catching and keeping livebaits. These days with many of our best bait-catching waters being intensively match- and pleasure-fished, bait catching is no longer easy. What's more, few angling clubs appreciate the pike angler helping themselves to their stock fish, even though the water is probably over-stocked and the fish growth reduced accordingly. The easy way round this problem is to buy your baits. Initially this may sound rather silly, but work it out; you normally pay for your deadbaits and to catch live-baits costs petrol and bait, while in many waters you risk being caught removing them, so buying your livebait can be less expensive than you think. Include the cost of your time spent bait catching instead of pike fishing and the economics of buying are obvious. The actual cost of the exercise depends on the size and species of bait and who you buy them from. Trout and roach of about 4 to 5 inches work out at about 20 to 30 pence each. A dozen is normally enough for most pike trips, so the cost is not prohibitive. If you do not live near to a fish supplier then you have to catch your own. Provided you have Water Authority permission the easiest way to obtain bait fish is to net a water, using a seine net. Syndicate waters and clubs which will allow this are not common, but if you have this opportunity you have it made. Fish traps are another method which can be very productive. The best fish to trap is the crucian carp. Waters where stunted crucians abound are common, particularly in East Anglia, the Midlands and the Northwest. For some reason crucians are absolute suckers for bread baited traps. Thrown into any area of a crucian pond, catch rates of 50 fish in an hour are quite possible. An evening session on a good water can produce enough for most of the

28¼lb Hollowell pike to a float paternostered live bream.

season. Tench and to a lesser extent common carp, are also susceptible to being trapped and even rudd and roach can sometimes be obtained using this method. Unfortunately the crucian and the perch (during the spring) are about the only guaranteed victims of a fish trap, unless the trap can be positioned in an area used by fish to move from one place to another.

Traps are generally made of chicken wire on a metal frame, though these days Netlon is much more acceptable due to the reduced damage to the bait fish. Traps need to be of only a modest size to work, 2 x 3 x 1½ feet being quite large enough. A funnel leads the fish in at one end while removal is facilitated by means of a door. Some of my traps are simple conversions of old keepnets and these seem to work very well. Whatever you do don't let people see you trapping or leave markers where your traps are. If you do, they will walk! Traps are best left for a couple of hours or at longest over-night. Hide the cord attaching them to the bank or better still throw them in unattached. A small grappling hook can then be used to retrieve them.

Another rather simple method, which can work really well on some waters, is to walk quietly round the margins of a lake at night and drag a large meshed landing net through the water at the edge. In heavily stocked ponds, small fish tend to move in very close to the edge at night and a landing net quickly scooped close to the bank or through a weed-bed can usually provide enough bait for a day's piking.

What of the terrible prospect of catching bait by rod and line? First, it pays to pick the right water. Small pits and pools, relatively unfished and full of rudd, are the answer to the pike man's prayer. In 60 minutes I have caught 90 two to four ounce rudd, all on float fished maggot on a 14-hook cast in among the visible shoals of fish. Still waters are generally a good bet in the autumn, but as it gets colder these waters in most cases go off. Then rivers and drains are the only hope. Well-stocked fen drains usually fish well when coloured and running off. In these conditions laying on with float tackle can produce suicidal bites from normally timid roach and bream. In clearer water the hour before dusk can be really productive. In rivers, bait can usually be caught easily when water conditions are normal. The air temperatures can be very low, but fish such as dace and chub are often willing feeders. The key to bait catching is to find the best waters, the best times and the best methods. Then with a bit of luck your visits need not be too long or too frequent. If you live in really heavily fished areas you may have to learn to fish properly. By this I mean with fine line and small hooks. Luckily I have seldom had to resort to such tactics, which is just as well.

One of the writer's fish traps. Made from an old mink trap and suitably modified with entrance cone and door.

The size of bait you use depends very much on what you can get hold of. My personal choice is to use baits of 2 to 6 ounces whenever possible. Only in dire circumstances do I go above these sizes. The advantages of small baits far outweighs any supposed advantages of big baits. You can keep more small baits in the same amount of water than you can big baits. Small baits produce a wider range of pike sizes and of course you miss fewer runs on them. Very, very occasionally, the pike in certain waters take it upon themselves to be fussy. They require a bigger than normal bait, say 8 to 10 ounces. In these circumstances I will obviously bend to the whims of the pike, but it is silly to fish large live-baits as a matter of habit.

With a little forethought it is quite easy to build up a stock of bait so that bait catching is eliminated for most of the early part of the winter. I have in fact kept baits such as chub and crucians from August right until the end of the season. The key to keeping a good stock of baits is clean, well-oxygenated water, without overcrowding. I situate my tanks outside at the back of the garage. The tanks are mainly fibre glass water cisterns of up to 50 gallons capacity. These sit on a gravel base which acts as a soakaway for excess water if no drain is nearby or on concrete or paving slabs if there is a drain near. The ideal system is to have some form of permanent through flow, particularly if you are keeping rainbow trout. An outside tap is preferable and then a trickle of water is run into the tank all the time. An overflow pipe in the side of the tank then takes the excess water to the drain or into a suitable soakaway. It is surprising how little throughflow is required to keep the water clean and of course it helps to prevent freezing during the winter, mains water being comparatively warm. If this arrangement is impossible, then it pays to exchange the water from time to time, usually with a hose and syphon. The water tends to get dirty when fresh fish are introduced, as they are still digesting food and excreting waste. Baits should never be fed unless a through flow is in use as this causes increased excretion which leads to a build up of waste products such as ammonia and fish don't like this. As far as aeration is concerned, you can never have too much. I always have two different air pumps leading to each tank. This provides some provision for failure of a pump. The air pumps I prefer are the diaphragm type made by Rena. Though there are other cheaper pumps which seem just as good, they always seem to expire after a year or so and fitting new parts is always difficult. The aerators are hung up in the garage and plastic air lines lead out to the tanks where square diffuser stones break the air stream up into fine bubbles. This increase in surface area is essential for rapid gas exchange and oxygenation of the water.

My livebait tank arrangement.

With two aerators leading to one 50 gallon tank it is possible to hold over 100 four ounce baits at temperatures of 15°C and obviously in colder weather and with the addition of through flow more baits can be kept. I normally run a couple of such tanks with baits graded according to size. I also keep a small tank for used baits so that they can be reused without mixing with fresh baits.

All tanks are covered by Netlon covers or wooden boards. Trout, chub and dace will jump out of anything! A little shade also helps to protect the fish from stress caused by being exposed. The biggest problem likely to be encountered by the livebait keeper is disease. White spot, fungus and bacterial infections which cause sores and dropsy are all likely to occur. Therefore never keep diseased fish and certainly never bring them in from elsewhere or take them to another water. Bacterial infections are particularly dangerous and you are better off killing the fish and treating the tanks with hypochlorate before starting again. White spot is only serious at high temperatures and fungus is usually only a problem in the winter. All diseases can be avoided to some extent by careful handling of the baits and removing suspect fish. Always put baits straight into the bucket and never use a keepnet. For transporting baits, use a fermenting bucket or one of those containers with a tight fitting lid used to hold paint or cooking oil. A hole in the lid is used to insert an air line and a portable aerator keeps them alive. At the water a second lid with ¼ inch holes in it can be fitted and the bin sunk. The baits stay alive and in the best possible condition this way. Alternatively a piece of netting can be fitted over the mouth of the bucket and held in place with an elastic strap.

The type of bait you choose to use is, as always, dependent on availability. The same fish species from two different waters can have different characteristics. Crucians are particularly like this; whilst most crucians give up the ghost and work very slowly in cold water, I once had some which went well at all times. Generally baits can be broken down into warm water and cold water baits. Those which go best in the autumn are rudd, crucians and carp. Winter baits are roach, common and silver bream, dace and chub. The reason I make these artificial divisions is to enable myself to have baits which actually swim around, not just lie doggo all the time. Similarly I don't want a bait which is too lively and tangles me up all the time. That is why my favourite autumn bait must be the crucian carp. They work really well and never tangle when fished on a paternoster. Rudd, though good workers, are just the opposite, they tangle everything up during the early part of the season and do nothing in the depth of the winter. There are of course many other baits you could use and I have tried most of them at one time or another. Pike are not really fussy about what sort of bait you chuck at them, as long as it swims a bit. Most of the time roach are the usual bait simply because roach are universally obtainable.

Once a steady supply of livebait is obtained the angler is free to consider how he intends to present his bait. The most effective method of presenting a livebait is without a doubt the float paternoster in any of its variations. If restricted to one method of pike fishing I think I would settle for this one above all others, yet each year you hear 'instant' pike experts knocking it in favour of perhaps more traditional and mobile methods. Though the free roving livebait fished a foot deep under a bung can be deadly on the right water at the right time, I am afraid the float paternoster beats it hands down in nearly all situations. There are a number of variations in the way it can be set up, and the diagrams hopefully explain these variations in detail. The method I use early in the season is a simple derivation of the standard paternoster as thought up by Rick Gibbinson. The paternoster tail is tied using a Billy Lane sliding float knot to the trace about halfway along. This serves to restrict the movement of the bait and prevents and up and over tangle which invariably results in a lost pike. Later in the season when bait activity is reduced I switch to the running paternoster. This allows a greater range of movement of the bait.

Livebait bin with tight fitting lid. The knotless net cover can be secured with an elastic strap over the bin mouth and placed in the water, thus keeping the baits lively.

Battery powered aerators. I use rechargeable batteries as these work out more economical in the long run. Rechargeable battery life of 5 to 6 hours.

Whether you choose to fish the float on the surface or sunken depends on the waters fished. If you fish a water with very varied depths or move between various different waters during a day, I would choose a sunken paternoster. The chore of moving the stop knot up and down is eliminated and precision casting is not required. In all other situations a float on the surface is preferable, because it allows you to observe the bait and judge how it is working. A close watch on the float will also tell you if a tangle is developing. Provided you have set the depth exactly, any tangling of the terminal tackle will result in the float sitting lower and lower in the water. I find that when using a 1½ inch pilot float or polystyrene ball it helps to paint half the float black or green and the other fluorescent red or 'blaze' as it seems to be called. The amount of upward (tangling) and downward movement can then be judged by the amount of black or green seen compared with the coloured part of the float.

Another thing which pays dividends is to check the bait at least once an hour. Even with anti-tangle paternoster rigs, some fish, particularly rudd and silver bream, seem to be able to tangle with astonishing ease. Checking regularly almost eliminates bite offs caused by up and overs.

Up and overs are frequently caused by lack of attention to the bait, presumably when things are going slowly. Usually when pike are taking you do not get time to develop tangles so take extra care when you are blanking. The only fish of the day might be just about to take your bait and bite through the line — bad for you and most definitely bad for the pike! The occasional pull on the line helps to keep things straight and also wakes the bait up. Runs so often come after a quick pull, that it is advisable to do this throughout a session.

The advantages of the paternoster are numerous. It allows a bait to be held in a limited area and avoids frequent recasting, which wastes bait and also temporarily removes the bait from the pike's attention. Paternostered baits can be made to hold out in running water or against the wind on windy days. Its disadvantages are that it has a limited casting range compared with the legered deadbait and it produces a characteristic type of bait movement which may eventually deter pike from taking on hard fished waters.

Though I have mentioned elsewhere that pike are not very bright, they can, it seems, turn their noses up at something obvious and the paternostered livebait tends to be just that. The bait is too easily seen, caught and avoided! As far as casting range is concerned the standard set up and a small bait can be punched out to about fifty yards with a backwind. Otherwise you must try and find a backwind and balloon a bait out. A paperclip attached to the paternoster bomb holds the hand-tied knot on a large round balloon — colour and Donald Duck cartoons are optional — then just drift out to the required distance and pull to release; very neat and effective. Unfortunately very strong baits tend to pull the balloon against the wind. Bryan Culley came up with the only brilliant idea of his life so far, and that was to put the bait to sleep before drifting it out. To do this required dunking in an anaesthetic solution for about 5 minutes. Half a teaspoon of Benzocaine (Ethyl-4-aminobenzoate) dissolved in 10ml of Acetone (obtained fromBDH Chemicals, Poole, England) in a gallon of water does the trick. The bait then revives once it is out there.

The amount of weight used on the paternoster tail depends on conditions and bait size. I generally use 1 ounce bombs which are home-made with wire rings instead of swivels. I believe in using weights of this size all the time rather than using the minimum of weight because I don't want to keep recasting baits unnecessarily or have them drift out of position. It is not very often that big pike fret over the odd half ounce of lead and then if resistance is causing problems I attend to it. Never anticipate problems, wait for them to happen! The paternoster link

SURFACE FLOAT PATERNOSTER

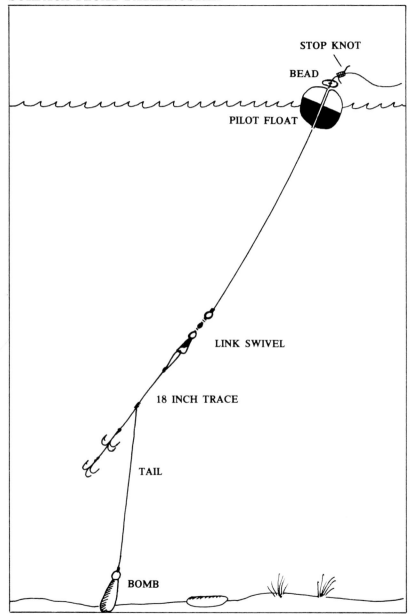

RUNNING PATERNOSTER

STANDARD PATERNOSTER

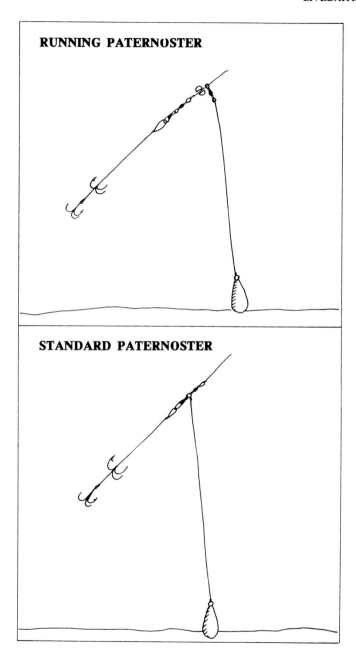

should be weaker than the main line, but only by a couple of pounds. We do not want to add additional lead to the environment.

By dispensing with the paternoster tail and adding a couple of swan shot above the trace we have a rig suitable for fishing a free swimming bait. It is essential to grease the line when doing this to make the line float and usually I use a rag smeared with Vaseline to run the line through. With a greased line it is sometimes possible to drift baits out without using a balloon. A vaned float can accelerate the process, but usually when the greased line is caught in a bow by the wind, progress is rapid enough. The free swimming bait is also useful for trotting in running water, though more lead is usually required to keep the bait down when checking its progress. I only use free swimming baits when there is some advantage to be gained by covering a wide area and when the wind is favourable. I have known days when pike seemed to prefer a free swimming bait to a paternostered one. The most recent was on the River Bure and though the pike caught were only small it was strange how they avoided the equally delicious paternostered baits in favour of the humble free swimming baits. On this hard fished water perhaps the different working action of the free swimming bait was more natural than the round and round, up and down of the paternostered bait.

If an even more natural presentation is desired, one can try the legered or freelined bait. Legered livebaits catch pike quite effectively on all sorts of waters and are easy to fish, provided one does not get too ambitious with the size of the bait. Livebaits of up to about four ounces are best for this work: anything bigger prevents you from keeping a tight line, simply because it gets up and swims around too much! Three different actions can be obtained from a legered livebait, simply by mounting it on the hooks in different ways. Head down with the top treble in the tail root and the second in the pelvic root, sees the bait trying to swim away from the rod tip, thus causing a fluttering action. Hooked head up the trace with the top treble through the lips, the bait tends to stay fairly still, while hooked in the back with the top treble the bait tends to lie on its side and constantly struggles to get upright. If it is variation one is looking for the legered livebait is worth considering. Hooking head up the trace gives you an edge when it comes to casting a long way and legered livebait can be put out remarkable distances provided the bait is small and the lead large (up to 3oz).

The freelined bait is, in my opinion, of limited value and comes into use only when fishing at close range with small baits or when fishing large active baits. A 10 ounce roach or bream can cover a lot of water on its own when not towing a lot of lead or floats around. It also tends to be

The best so far: a Norfolk Broad thirty. Weight 32.02, length 44 inches.

the most natural presentation of all and one I would recommend when fishing difficult waters. Its main disadvantage is its requirement for constant attention and it is very hard work controlling a bait for more than a couple of hours. If and when I use this method, it is usually around specific known feeding times on the waters I fish.

There are a few other variations of the basic themes already mentioned and though not really standard methods they can all be tried, perhaps in experimentation rather than in the hope of superior results to other methods. When larger baits are in short supply, two small baits can be fished on the same treble or on a specially designed twin hook rig first popularised by Martin Gay. Legered baits of a more conventional nature can be retrieved along the bottom thus covering more ground.

When I recently did a desk study of all my pike captures over 12 pounds and the bait used to catch them I was surprised to notice that livebaits accounted for 48.8% of the twenties, and deadbaits 51.2%. Of the fish of 15 pounds and over up to 20 pounds, 51.4% on lives and 48.6% on deads, and for fish of 12 to 15 pounds, 48% on livebaits and 52% on deadbaits. Looking at the data realistically, there is obviously no size selection, at least for double figure pike, and the numbers of pike over twelve pounds to live and deadbaits are almost the same. I always

Another Hollowell pike, this time of 26 pounds taken on a live roach.

fish both live and deadbaits though I might fish two deadbaits to one livebait where this is allowed. Overall this might mean that livebaits are slightly more effective than deadbaits for unit effort. This means that the pike angler who wants to fish seriously has to give serious consideration to the use of livebait. I am sure that a good lure angler or a deadbait wobbler could pick up some of the livebait-caught pike, but my own experiences convince me that on average livebaits are essential for all-round success.

My best Broadland pike of the 1982/83 season: 24.08. Note the slight parrot nose.

6 Deadbaiting

Of all the methods used while pike fishing, deadbaiting is probably the most versatile and also the most misunderstood. Deadbaiting is subject to more misconceptions than any other piking method and many pike fall to deadbaits, in spite of some of the peculiar logic which prompts the pike angler to use the method. It has been accused of being 'slow', a 'lazy man's method of fishing', 'likely to result in deep hooked pike' and 'selective for big pike', because big pike are too old, slow and lazy to chase food. To put it bluntly, all of this is a load of shoe menders! Just like any other form of fishing, in the long term you only get out what you put in. Also, before you make any of the above conclusions it pays to fish around a bit and catch pike from a wide selection of waters, using a variety of deadbaiting methods.

As mentioned in Chapter 5, deadbaits account for about half of my big pike. I suspect also that between 40% and 50% of my smaller pike also fall to deadbaits. Though it is true that some waters are poor deadbait waters, it is also true that this is balanced by other waters which actually respond best to deadbaiting. The habits of pike can also change from day to day or from season to season. A few years ago the Sixteen Foot drain was a noted livebait water, and deadbaits, particularly sea baits such as herrings and mackerel, tended to be very slow compared with livebaits. Livebaits were also producing more, and larger, pike than dead baits. Recently however, this has all changed and sea fish baits have been scoring almost to the exclusion of livebaits. This was evidenced by some really strange captures. One November Dave Phillips was trying out a new swim he had fancied for some time. He tried a small pike livebait and the obligatory half mackerel legered in the same swim. For some time the small pike went mad; something appeared to be spooking it. Nothing took it, but the half mackerel went away and a 21 pounder was landed. Similar events have befallen me so many times on some waters that one wonders whether livebaiting is worthwhile. Just every so often the pike have a change and the reverse occurs. It is being able to score on those odd days which fills the log book with big pike rather than blanks!

Pike pick up deadbaits because they recognise them as being food. I doubt if they can think: 'H'm, this is a nice easy meal, I think I will take this in preference to that shoal of roach over there!' If they see it and

31.14 Irish Lough pike: Spring 1982.

happen to be hungry, they take it. In some waters pike are so pre-occupied with catching live fish, they ignore deadbaits. Such pike need an additional stimulus to invoke a feeding response and that stimulus is movement. Small pike are particularly prone to this form of behaviour and this is why very small pike are more often taken on livebaits rather than deadbaits on some waters. It seems that pike are not so exacting in their requirement for movement as they get larger. This may be because young pike instinctively react to movement, from the time they first start to feed. This snapping response is very common in young salmonids and something fish farmers try to encourage when they first start to feed fry on artificial food by putting the food in near the inflow thus making it move and stimulating the response. The requirement for movement soon fades and the young trout or salmon learn to take static food. As pike grow they obviously encounter dead fish in the environment and before long they have 'realised' that dead fish are fair game. Poor dead-bait waters may be waters where very few dead fish are encountered, and, similarly, good deadbait waters may be waters where they are common. Sometimes there is no obvious explanation for changes in preference from live to deadbaits and then the explanation may lie in Barrie Rickards' theory that pike move to livebaits and lures more readily in periods of anticyclonic (high pressure) and to deadbaits during prolonged cyclonic (low pressure) conditions. Unfortunately on many waters other factors override any influence that barometric pressure might have. However, if you are concentrating on one particular water for a whole season and the pike appear to follow barometric pressure trends, then it might well be worth adapting your fishing methods accordingly. For the most part the pike's preference for live or deadbait appears to be beyond our understanding, this being a good reason for always fishing live and deadbaits!

On waters where the pike are long, lean and hungry, deadbaits are usually a very good method, but, as I mentioned earlier, preoccupation with shoals of prey fish can lead to static deadbaits being ignored. In September of 1981 I made an 18 fish catch for 130 odd pounds from a Midland water, all on livebaits or wobbled deadbaits. Static baits were totally ignored, but try winding one in and bang, a pike! I even had a sixteen pounder on half a twaite shad, along with others on more conventional variations of the wobbled deadbait. Yet these pike were long and lean and feeding like mad. They were obviously turned on by movement and to the exclusion of deadbaits sitting on the bottom.

Static deadbaiting with the bait fished on the bottom can be a slow game, but there are equally many, many occasions when things have been far from slow. I have had many catches of up to a dozen pike, with up to five doubles included, all on deadbaits. The most notable day ever was in Ireland during Easter of 1981. In order of appearance the following fish came to my rods: 12.14, 25.04, 20.06, 24.00, 9.08 and 16.10. All these fish were caught on half mackerel, half trout or half roach baits. Days like this can hardly be described as slow! A lot depends on the waters you fish. Fishing a poor deadbait water with static deadbaits is bound to result in an overdose of boredom. The angler has to pick the right types of waters or be much more flexible in his approach. By learning where and when to use the various forms and presentations of deadbaits, deadbaiting can be improved to the point at which it should account for a large proportion of the pike caught. To me this is important for a number of reasons. On many waters pike anglers no longer have the option to livebait. While I disagree strongly with bans of this sort, one has to fall into line on waters where you are in full view of other anglers and this means that one has to deadbait effectively. Deadbaiting is also much easier than livebaiting because there are no bait to catch, transport or look after. Tangles and mishaps are less numerous. By fishing both live and deadbaits one also tends to reduce the number of livebaits required and this in turn allows more fishing time spent after pike rather than 'liveos'.

If the very thought of sitting still for more than an hour gives you apoplexy then the mobile methods of wobbled deadbaiting or drifting baits are perhaps for you. However there is no guarantee that these methods will be any less boring and I don't recommend them in the rain! As far as static deadbaiting being a lazy man's fishing, it really is a case of how you approach your fishing. Just like anyone I have my off days when casting a deadbait out and putting it on a buzzer is the sum total of my effort. A good book then relieves the boredom while I wait for a run. Fortunately things are not always like this, and usually a positive approach, which involved moving baits or swims, produces far more fish. The point to realise is that the angler's mood and the pike's mood influence the way you fish. If the weather is miserable and the pike apathetic, I will not enjoy myself sitting in the rain or snow, moving swims or rowing around in a boat, so I either go home or sit tight under the brolly. I go fishing to enjoy myself, not as an endurance test. Anyone who can persevere in really bad conditions is, of course, a lucky man and can derive a tremendous amount of satisfaction from catching a good fish on a bad day. Most of the time, however, the hardy types blank anyway!

Deadbaiting can be a slow game . . . .

Deep hooking is not really an attribute of deadbaiting, but rather a problem caused by failing to judge when a pike has the bait in its mouth rather than its throat. I doubt if there is any real difference in the number of deep hooked fish between live and deadbaiting and anyway this is not really a problem as I have noted earlier.

Much as in livebaiting, there is a varied choice of baits that the angler can use. I have probably tried as wide a variety of deadbaits as anyone.in the hope of finding the magic bait which outfishes all others. At the moment it seems that the ultimate bait does not exist. All baits have their day and some seem to be better than others on some waters. However, in the final reckoning no bait is infallible and it seems that pike will take virtually any type of deadbait on the right day. I do not believe that pike are that good at discriminating between different baits and certainly when using similar types of bait I have been hard pressed to find any significant preference for one or another. I do believe that pike can be choosey when two very different baits are being used. Deadbaits can be loosely divided into two categories, sea fish baits and freshwater baits (which I term as naturals, for pike may encounter such fish in the wild, while herrings and the like are not likely to be encountered naturally). Sea fish baits include a limited number of fish which belong to either the herring or the mackerel family. These include herrings, sprats, sardines, mackerel and scad or horse mackerel. All these fish tend to have very oily flesh and smell very different from natural baits. Natural baits include all the freshwater fish found in this country, and smelt and trout, although there are other sea fish such as whiting, snappers, gurnard, grey and red mullet and garfish, which have all caught pike, I do not use them. One reason is the price of some of the exotic baits, the other is the poor availability. Therefore I concentrate my efforts on baits which are usually easily obtained and fairly cheap. I am not convinced that the more exotic baits have any value as change baits and feel that if you cannot catch on the usual natural and sea fish baits you are not going to catch anyway. Natural baits, though differing considerably in size, colour and shape, appear to me at least (with the exception of grayling and smelt) to have very similar smells, so that the pike is unlikely to choose one rather than another, at least on the basis of smell alone, though other factors such as colour and shape might have some influence here.

A vital piece of equipment for the keen pike angler is a deep freeze. Pike do not seem to worry much about taking frozen bait, even while they are still hard! The advantage of freezing baits is such that a keen pike angler could do worse than to have a freezer for his deadbaits alone, thus avoiding having to rummage amongst the peas and sprouts. Deadbaits can be bought in bulk from wholesale outlets at much reduced prices and for seasonal baits like sprats, stocks can be built up for the whole year. Coarse fish baits are usually dead livebaits and in this way nothing is wasted. I have never had to go out and specifically catch coarse fish for the freezer, due to using the dead livebaits, even those rescued from the pike's jaws.

My deep freeze is a standard model, but ice cream freezers and the like can be bought for much less. In order to be able to select exactly which baits you want for a day's fishing, some care is required in wrapping and packing. I always freeze my baits individually. Small baits are laid out on baking trays covered with a polythene bag. When frozen the individual baits can then be bagged and placed into those 4 litre ice cream containers my garage seems to be full of. Larger baits are packed in layers in the freezer in a similar manner and then bagged when frozen. Baits are layered in the freezer so that some of each are always on the top; this saves digging around. Wrapping helps to prevent dehydration of the baits, for they can lose a lot of water over a year. Baits keep like this for at least a year and I have had pike on baits of a considerably earlier vintage than this. For transport to the water I use a freezer box and freezer blocks. In this way wastage is avoided and unused baits can be returned to the freezer. For long walks I usually wrap a few baits up in newspaper and leave the box under a sack in the van, safe in the knowledge that should I run out of bait I have some left in reserve. On each trip I always take both sea and natural baits for there are days when one is preferred to the other and I have no intention of getting caught out, even though it does mean more bait to lug around.

As far as static deadbaiting is concerned it pays to try to change baits during the day. A pike might be tempted by a larger or a smaller bait, or a sea fish rather than a natural. Generally I have noticed that pike will show a preference for one size of bait or between sea and freshwater baits. This is why having access to sardines and sprats as well as herrings and mackerel is so useful. You can give the pike a choice of sizes of whole baits. Similarly a natural can be substituted for a sea fish bait or vice versa. There are unfortunately no hard and fast rules which indicate when to do what. It is very much a case of learning the hard way. Some things are fairly obvious. If you miss runs it pays to use smaller baits. If the pike are wolfing baits you can perhaps step up the size of the bait.

Looking at my results, on average I catch about the same number of pike on natural and sea fish baits. This is not surprising as I tend to use both about the same amount. So, over a wide range of different waters, both types are equally effective. However this is only 'on average'. Some waters are very biased towards sea fish baits or naturals. This can result in almost nil results to one and everything on the other!

Another factor which should not be overlooked is the versatility of the bait during fishing. For long distance work, the head or tail of the mackerel takes some beating. Provided the bait is nice and straight when frozen solid, about 4 to 6 ounces, and matched to a suitable rod, distances of 80 yards are quite possible. Indeed Dave Phillips once came under fire while fishing in fog opposite Barrie Rickards on the Relief Channel. Few of us can do the ton as Barrie has, but for most purposes 80 yards is good enough. Herrings are not quite so good, but the head half of an 8 to 10oz roach runs the half mackerel a close second. The rather unstreamlined shape is dense enough to give a lot of casting weight and it tends to run 'clean' on the cast. If a large natural bait has to be fished well out, the half roach fits this requirement. Sardines and sprats are only really viable as long range baits when frozen, due to disintegration. Sardines, especially, fall to bits if cast out hard. However when frozen and used with a big lead, distance is no object. The same can be said for small naturals. Smelt and trout are good tough baits and

Freezer box and freezer blocks for keeping the deadbaits frozen.

can, with a backwind, be put out over 60 yards. Other baits are less versatile, except perhaps for a good-sized chunk of eel, which has probably brained the odd passing swan on some waters.

DEADBAITING HOOKING RIGS

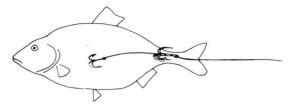

1. WHOLE DEADBAIT — TWO TREBLES WITH ONE HOOKED IN ROOT OF TAIL, OTHER HALFWAY ALONG BODY.

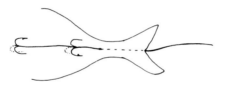

2. LONGER CASTING RIG, WITH TRACE THREADED THROUGH TAIL ROOT WITH BAITING NEEDLE.

3. TRACE TIED TO TAIL ROOT FOR LONG CASTING.

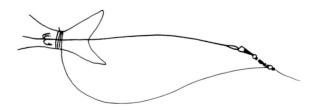

4. LINE TIED TO TAIL ROOT — TRACE NOT ATTACHED TO TAIL. LINE ENABLES BAIT TO BE RECOVERED FOR RE-USE.

5. SARDINE RIG. LARGE SINGLE (SIZE 1) HOOKED THROUGH EYE SOCKETS TAKES SHOCK OF CASTING. ALSO USED WITH SPRATS. FOR VERY SMALL BAITS DISPENSE WITH TREBLE.

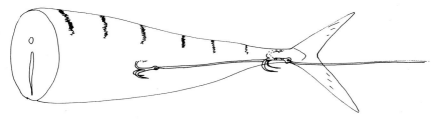

6. HALF MACKEREL WITH TANDEM TREBLES. SAME RIG FOR ALL HALF BAITS OF 2-6 OUNCES.

All of the baits I use regularly have proved themselves to some extent, but I do not try and attach too much significance to the bait used unless an obvious trend develops on a particular water. Many of the big pike below would probably have accepted an alternative bait if they had come across it first.

SOME BIG PIKE ON DEADBAITS

Weight	Bait
26.00	Sardine
27.14	Dead perch
25.04	Half roach
20.01	Half pike
24.14	Half mackerel
22.08	Whole herring
28.07	Half herring
21.00	Whole mackerel
25.04	Sprat
32.02 & 31.14	Smelt
23.12	Dead rudd
25.01	Dead roach

The deadly smelt deadbait.

Fresh sardines, a very soft, but particularly tasty bait!

I am very fond of the cucumber smelling smelt and certainly rate it very highly, especially as I caught my first thirty on one. However I have never really given it a fair trial against any similar baits, so I dare not make any rash claims about its effectiveness. All I know is, that I have a lot of confidence in smelt deadbaits, and have caught several good twenties on them plus a lot of big doubles, which is to my mind good enough a reason to keep using them. The desire to fish cucumber smelling baits led me down some very devious trails in the early seventies. I spent some time soaking my herrings in cucumber juice and first time out it worked with a 21.6 pike and my only zander ever to take a whole herring! Sadly the follow-up trials never produced much, even my efforts in biochemistry while at college failing to help. Using sophisticated equipment I tried to isolate the smell, but sadly it was beyond me to identify what exactly made cucumbers and smelts smell the way they do!

Flavours and colours have only been studied in a limited way by pike anglers and there is the possibility that deadbaits can be made more attractive. Red herrings and pilchard oil injected baits have all caught pike, some of them good ones. I had my first pike in 1982 on smoked mackerel and a 17.15 in 1983 on half a kipper. All this is good fun and adds to the interest of pike fishing. I am certainly not going to discount the possibilities of making baits a little different though so far my experiments have not resulted in any significant increase in catches compared with conventional baits. Certainly the smell of something like a smoked mackerel is such that a pike would be hard pressed not to notice it.

Actually fishing the static deadbait is a fairly simple process and provided one is attentive to small details, little can go wrong. Whenever possible I try to float leger my deadbaits. The float tells you which way the pike is heading, allows a greater spread of rods and most important of all, keeps the line off the bottom and most of the time out of snags. By paying attention to your floats a run can be detected as soon as a pike takes provided you are not fishing excessively overdepth. I normally aim to have the trace on the bottom of the swim with the uptrace weight holding everything in position. Any movement of the bait is transferred to the float and on calm days in particular it is often possible to notice very tentative movements which precede a full blooded run.

Terminal tackles are the inevitable two trebles for baits over 5 inches and a single and a treble for smaller baits. Very small baits can be presented on one single through the eye sockets. Simplicity is the key and generally I insert one treble in the tail root and the other in the flank. For long casting with soft baits which are not frozen it is worth threading the bait through the bone near the tail. PVA (Poly Vinyl Alcohol) thread or tape can be used to reinforce the hook hold on the bait. Alternatively, especially when bait is running short, the bait can be tied round the tail with 10lb nylon. In this way the bait comes back every time. Slightly more elaborate is tying a piece of line to the tail root before putting on the hooks and then tying it to the trace swivel. When the pike ejects the bait, the bait tied to the line comes back again! None of these dodges appear to have any effect on hooking efficiency, so it is up to the angler which he prefers.

Only when I am fairly sure that snags are unlikely to be encountered do I leger baits. Freelining has very little application in my fishing. Rigs are again very simple, either two or more swan shot pinched up trace, or a running lead of usually one ounce, sometimes more, sometimes less. Weight is always sufficient either to get the bait out to where it is wanted or to keep it there in wind and current. Movement is not required and frequently one wants to keep that bait in a limited area, so use whatever it takes.

END RING SLIDER FLOAT LEGER

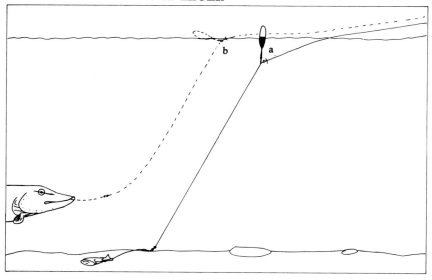

a. NORMAL BAIT PRESENTATION WHEN DEADBAITING.
b. PIKE PICKS UP BAIT AND FLOAT FALLS FLAT.

A variation of the static deadbait is the air-injected bait. I do not like the idea of polystyrene inserts being ingested by pike so I restrict my flotation methods to air and sometimes a small piece of cork attached to one prong of a treble. Such baits are useful where bottom weed is likely to obscure the bait, though pike are quite capable of finding well-hidden baits. Another simpler approach is simply to suspend the bait under a float either using a paternoster rig or a simple float fishing rig. Deadbaits of any type will take pike when suspended. I prefer sprats and dead naturals, but there is no reason not to try half mackerel or any other bait. How you suspend the bait depends on how far you need to cast. Mounted head down and tied on, long casts are quite easily achieved and the presentation is in no way unnatural as roach and bream in particular spend periods hanging head down in the water, with little movement. For shorter casts, bait can be mounted to fish horizontally and for running water, head up trace. The suspended deadbait is a rather neglected method and I must admit to failing to give it as much attention as it deserves. This I will rectify because in some situations it is a very good substitute for a float fished livebait. More than once I have known pike to take suspended deadbaits in preference to livebaits and one day on the River Delph when 5 fish took deadbaits suspended to one on livebait, I actually ended up killing one livebait to get a run on it! Experience has shown that in some circumstances, particularly when a water has been flogged with livebaits, a suspended deadbait will produce more pike. This is, I am sure, due to the livebaits 'unnatural' erratic actions. A suspended deadbait would appear to be nothing more than a fish suspended in the water, a perfectly natural phenomenon.

Wobbled deadbaits perhaps deserve more attention than I am going to give them here, but because I do so little deadbait wobbling, their part in this chapter must be rather small. Though I have had pike to 21¾lb on mobile deadbaits, their greatest use seems to be in locating pike. By working along a drain or round a pit, takes or follow ups can

WOBBLED DEADBAIT

TANDEM TREBLES — ONE THROUGH TOP AND BOTTOM LIPS, OTHER IN FLANK — TO GIVE 'KINK' FOR WOBBLING ACTION.

lead to the identification of new swims. For most of my deadbait wobbling I use sprats and small roach. These are mounted simply on two trebles, one in the head, the other in the flank. Depending on how the pike want the bait on the day, the amount of curvature imparted to the bait can be varied by the positioning of the second treble. For larger baits more complex rigs may have to be devised, with as many as three trebles in use. A few years ago such rigs were very much in vogue, but today I think most pike anglers try and avoid multi-hook rigs due to the potential for damaging the pike.

Usually some weight is required uptrace to get the bait to fish near the bottom. A couple of swan shot is usually all that is required, though an anti-kink lead is very useful when trolling. This is simply a half moon shaped piece of lead sheet folded over the line above the trace. Sometimes you do not need to fish the bait near the bottom and this is particularly true in the summer, when you are trying to extract pike from weedy areas. Much of what applies to deadbait wobbling also applies to lure fishing, so I will leave Trevor Moss to deal with this.

There is always something special about a good fast deadbait run — the excitement of not knowing whether the pike is a big one or just another micropike, although in some waters deadbaits are very selective for big pike, particularly when using sea fish baits. There are many waters where deadbaits catch all sizes of pike. On waters where deadbaits are selective, you can wait a long time for a run. On the other hand action can be fast and furious, with lots of small fish, with the odd big one thrown in. Though deadbaiting has something of a chuck it and chance it reputation I hope that in some of the following sections this image is to some extent shattered.

7 Lure Fishing

'Lure fishing for pike is a method of limited application to most pike fishing situations.' This statement, though somewhat sweeping, sums up my outlook on lure fishing. Though I have caught a fair number of pike up to 13 pounds on lures and enjoy using artificials in the right circumstances, I see no point in trying to make them work when other methods are usually superior.

Despite this rather negative outlook, I have every intention of catching a big pike on a lure, one day. I suspect that Ireland offers the best chance of achieving this aim. In the meantime I have asked lure enthusiast Trevor Moss to write the chapter on lure fishing.

Neville Fickling

LURES — by TREVOR MOSS

Before commencing this chapter I would like to place one or two points in the right context: firstly I would like to make it quite clear to the reader that I do not consider myself any sort of an expert or successful catcher of big pike on lures, and this short contribution to Neville's book is more of a guide to what types of lures are available to the pike angler, plus some of their uses. Having said that, I do feel qualified in the sense that I am one of the few retailers in the fishing tackle trade that has gone some way to specializing in supplying American lures for the pike angler.

On the practical side my introduction to the merits of American lures happened some twenty odd years ago with one of our local, now disused, RAF bases being taken over by the American Air Force. My mother, along with many other local women, found civilian employment there, and consequently my parents became friends of American families stationed there. American airman Gordon Ellis introduced me to the delights of pike fishing with lures and he remains a family friend to this day. He is now retired from the USAF and is living with his family in Kimbolton, Bedfordshire.

One of our favourite venues at that time was a small picturesque lake called Norton Place which at the time was teeming with small pike. We used to fish surface lures for them; red and white 'Poppers' about

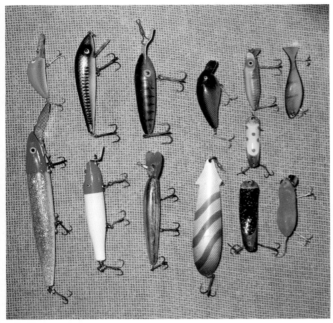

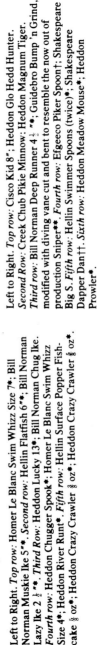

Left to Right. *Top row:* Homer Le Blanc Swim Whizz Size 7*; Bill Norman Muskie Ike 5*; Hellin Flatfish 6**; Bill Norman Lazy Ike 2 ½ "*. *Third Row:* Heddon Lucky 13*; Bill Norman Chug Ike. *Fourth row:* Heddon Chugger Spook*; Homer Le Blanc Swim Whizz Size 4*; Heddon River Runt*. *Fifth row:* Hellin Surface Popper Fishcake ⅝ oz*; Heddon Crazy Crawler ⅜ oz*; Heddon Crazy Crawler ⅝ oz*.

* Lures which Trevor Moss has caught pike on.
** Neville Fickling has taken the odd pike on this lure and it works well trolled.
† Neville Fickling has taken quite a few pike on this spoon up to 11 pounds.
†† Neville's best pike on one of these weighed 13 ½ lb.

Left to Right. *Top row:* Cisco Kid 8"; Heddon Glo Hedd Hunter. *Second Row:* Creek Chub Pikie Minnow: Heddon Magnum Tiger. *Third row:* Bill Norman Deep Runner 4 ½ "*; Guidebro Bump 'n Grind, modified with diving vane cut and bent to resemble the now out of production Sniper**. *Fourth row:* Efgeeco Piker Spoon†; Shakespeare Big S. *Fifth row:* Hellin Swimmer Spoons (twice)*; Shakespeare Dapper Dan††. *Sixth row:* Heddon Meadow Mouse*; Heddon Prowler*.

All other lures have been proved to be effective pike catchers. The Big S in particular has a large number of Irish 'twenties' to its credit. Dennis Smith of Peterborough caught the biggest Rutland water pike of 1981 on a Cisco Kid, 28 ¼ lb. Gordon Burton of Southport has had a number of big Scottish pike on the Creek Chub Pikie.

2 inches long with a little propeller at the tail that gurgled as the lure was retrieved. Mepps spinners were another favourite but we used to fix a short length of obnoxious-smelling coloured 'pork rind' to one of the treble points, to make the spinner more attractive. I can still clearly remember the fabulous takes we used to get from those little pike; all text book stuff—pike shooting out of the reed beds like torpedoes, hitting our lures with such ferocity that they often came clear of the water, with the lure firmly embedded in their jaws!

Since those early days I have always kept a good space in my tackle box for a number of my favourite lures. My lure fishing nowadays is purely fun fishing. The size of fish doesn't come into it, and I find a few summer evenings down at the local gravel pits very enjoyable, but all my serious pike fishing is now confined to the winter months with standard live and deadbait techniques.

Are Lures a Proficient Method of Catching Big Pike?

On certain waters lures can be a deadly method of catching pike throughout the warmer months of the year. From spring, through to the end of October, I would rate as the best time for successful lure fishing. Of course there are plenty of pike taken on lures during the winter months, but my own preferences for that time of year would be more suited to live and dead bait methods. Wobbled deadbaits would replace any free roving lure fishing.

Lure fishing was popularised in the 60's by the exploits of Fred Wagstaff and Bob Reynolds to name just two of the many successful lure fishing fanatics of that era. More recently anglers such as Gordon Burton of Southport and southern pike specialist Steve Tolan, regularly catch large pike on artificial lures from the lochs of Scotland, the large Southern gravel pits and reservoirs. So yes, lures can be a proficient method of catching big pike. The members of the Northern Ireland Pike Society also catch a lot of big pike on lures.

Personally I don't think the pike angler who decides to lure fish in exclusion to any other method would be anything like as successful, big fish-wise, as the more versatile pike angler, using all the methods available throughout the year.

Waters Most Likely to Respond to Lure Fishing Methods

You could say, perhaps, that every type of pike water at sometime has yielded some of its pike to the angler who has tossed out a plug, or spinner, whether purposely approached or just an angler whiling away half an hour because things were a bit slow, and he fancied a walk round to relieve, dare I say it, his boredom. One has only to read the angling press to find captions such as '9 year old boy lands 20lb pike on home-made plug' etc. These type of stories make the pike angler prick up his ears, but these one-off fish don't mean that the water is a good prospect for lure fishing. My own experiences lead me to think that there are no hard and fast rules. To evaluate a bit further, one large gravel pit on the outskirts of Lincoln once produced a big catch of pike subsequently reported to the angling press as being caught on a pike bung. Apparently this enterprising angler was using a livebait suspended under a pike bung and, while he was fishing, his float was constantly being attacked by pike. Using his initiative he removed the livebait and rigged up a trailing treble attached to the float, twitched it across the surface and took a fair catch of pike; one of them a fair-sized double if my memory serves me correctly. I fished this water many times after reading about this angler's success, with various types of surface lures, and can honestly say that I have never had a fish take a lure off the surface on this water, although I and other members of Witham Valley Specimen Group caught a fair number of pike from this particular water on live and dead baits; perhaps I should have used a pike bung!

Any waters where pike are seen to strike regularly on the surface should prove to be good lure waters, particularly to surface type lures such as Heddon Crazy Crawlers that work along the surface, and shallow working lures like the Heddon Lucky 13 that float and, when retrieved, work just under the surface. These lures are very successful on shallow weedy waters worked very slowly over and round the weed beds. I have a particular fancy for the 4" Lucky 13 and have a silver coloured scar-ridden one, that must be at least 20 years old, made from wood, that has caught plenty of pike for me over the years. I am now thinking of retiring it for fear of losing it. Like most lures now the Lucky 13 is made of plastic; they still work well but don't cast like the old wooden ones.

Clear weedy gravel pits with plenty of features would always be my first choice as plug fishing waters. The same applies to lakes and reservoirs. I have never personally had confidence in the murky type of water. I have taken pike from the Witham and its drains on lures but much prefer to stick to wobbled baits and standard live and dead bait techniques on this type of water. Although the Witham is usually very clear in summer, my fishing on the river is restricted to the winter months, due to my attention being with other species of fish in the summer. The pike I have had on lures have been taken in early October before the river has fully taken on its murky winter colour.

Of course the Mecca for the lure angler is the vast lochs of Scotland such as Lomond and Awe, and the many loughs of Ireland. These waters need a very specialised approach with lures and in no way am I qualified to advise the angler on how to fish them. My very limited experience is on Loch Awe and Lomond trolling lures using a lead core line rig. The rig I use works well in theory, but as for personal successes the numbers of fish taken using the method is best left unmentioned! The trolling rig is quite simple: a wide drum centre pin loaded with 25lbs BS braided mono (approx. 200 yards); spliced to the mono is 18 yards of 30lb lead core trolling line with the joint subsequently whipped over with fly tying thread and varnished. At the business end of the trolling line I attach a short length of 15lb Sylcast (approx. 24″) and to this a 12″ wire trace made from 18lb pike strand trace wire with a Berkley swivel and Berkley snap swivel attached to the line.

DEEP TROLLING RIG

15lb LINE

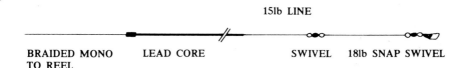

BRAIDED MONO   LEAD CORE   SWIVEL   18lb SNAP SWIVEL
TO REEL

To fish the rig simply pay out the desired amount of line, letting the lead core get down to the required depth; set the boat moving very slowly, preferably rowed. Obviously this rig cannot be used by oneself, someone needs to row or work the motor. Work the rig along a previously mapped out route such as gravel bars or sharp drop-offs, round islands etc. For anglers not possessing an echo sounder the Admiralty chart map of Loch Lomond may prove very useful; this chart gives all the depths contours of the loch at normal summer water levels.

The Lures and Their Uses

The availability of American lures in England is fairly limited. 90% of all the American lures available from tackle dealers such as myself originate from Ken Latham of Potter Heigham in Norfolk. Ken in the 60's was a fanatical lure angler, fishing the then prolific Norfolk Broads. With lure fishing becoming popularised through the writings of Wagstaff and Reynolds, Ken decided to set up a company called Ken Latham's American Lure Imports. He imported vast quantities of all the popular American lures. Names like Lazy Ike, Burkes Lures, Helins, Creek Chub, Heddon, Bill Norman and Cisco Kid became available to the British pike angler. Unfortunately, with the decline in the quality of the pike fishing on the Broads, due mainly to prymnesium and firms making cheap inferior copies of American lures, plus the general decline in the popularity of lure fishing, Ken decided to draw a halt to his American imports. The lures available today are just remnants of Ken's once fantastic stock of lures, all except Heddon which Ken once again is importing on a regular basis.

Lure fishing is now increasing in popularity so perhaps Ken in the future may decide to top up his dwindling stocks of Creek Chub, Cisco Kid lures etc, indeed the British lure angler is greatly indebted to Ken Latham.

Lures

The word 'lure' must certainly originate from the USA and even the non-angler must connect it with something to do with fishing. The English counterpart name of 'plug' to me sounds ridiculous, and to anyone but an angler it most certainly would be regarded as something electrical or a thing you put in the sink! Though lures are made from wood, plastic or metal, and may revolve, float or wobble, they all serve the same basic purpose, to deceive the quarry into thinking what is being presented to them is food, whether it's pike, perch, trout or chub that the angler may be seeking.

The following is a list of lures that I have personally been successful with, or friends who lure fish have had success with. They are listed in categories, lures that float and work on the surface or just below the surface, lures that float and when retrieved dive down to a medium depth, and thirdly lures that sink or deep dive. I have given a brief description with each section:

Surface and shallow working lures (floating) plastic

Heddon Crazy Crawler — Available in two sizes $\frac{5}{8}$ oz and $\frac{1}{4}$ oz. Works directly on the surface. Very effective on shallow weedy water. Small flippers on the sides of the lure create a splashy walking effect.

Heddon Meadow Mouse — $\frac{1}{2}$oz. An excellent imitation, works directly on the surface or just below depending on retrieve speed.

Heddon Lucky 13 — 4″ size. Works just below the surface. Little surface swirls and splashes can be created by twitching the rod tip.

Heddon Prowler — $\frac{3}{8}$oz. Imitates injured fish. Will work down to a depth of approximately 2 feet.

Helins Surface Popper Fishcake — wood $\frac{3}{8}$oz. Who else but the USA could come up with a name like that! Gurgles across the surface with the aid of small rotating propeller at the front of the lure. This ridiculous looking lure has on numerous occasions proved very effective.

Burkes Top Water Pop Top — $\frac{3}{8}$oz. Soft latex material. This very effective surface lure is designed with a dished-in face to create a bubbling effect when retrieved. This lure, I think, is now no longer available in the UK.

Bomber Jerk — wood $\frac{7}{8}$oz. Works just under the surface, should be fished in a slow jerky fashion.

Creek Chub Mouse — wood. Works just under the surface. Is smaller than the Heddon Mouse and is available in day glow fluorescent colours.

Lures that float and when retrieved dive to a medium depth

Shakespeare Big 'S', Middy 'S' and Little 'S' — I have grouped these together as all have proved very effective for me. They are a very appetizing looking lure, humped back with a fat belly. They always remind me of a pregnant goldfish. All these sizes have a rattle but I will leave it to the experts to argue whether the rattle makes any difference to its pike-catching abilities!

Homer le Blanc Swim Whizz — plastic. This lure is available in three sizes: 4″, 6″ and a giant trolling size 7″. The 4″ and 6″ sizes are superb —they have two trace attachment points, one makes the lure fish shallow, the other allows it to be fished down to about four feet. The lure has a superb action and has accounted for many pike.

Lazy Ike, Musky Ike — wood/newer model plastic. 5″ long and slightly banana shaped, this lure has not been successful for me personally but friends have taken pike on it. Its size and shape certainly make it an effective-looking lure and will work down to about 5′ deep.

Creek Chub Straight Pikie Minnow — wood. The 6″ Pikie Minnow looks just like a small pike. Fishes with a slow lazy action. Works down to about 5′ depending on speed of retrieve.

The Heddon Crazy Crawler, in action.

Most of the lures in the last section can be made to work deeper than I have suggested by adding weight. A simple way to do this is shown in the diagram. I recommend the swivel to be the ball-bearing type which helps to alleviate the line twisting.

Lures that sink or spin or dive very deep

Bill Norman Deep Runner — alloy metal. This lure is one of the deepest working lures I have used. My 4½″ model has proved very useful on a big Nottinghamshire gravel pit. Its dart-like shape makes long casting easy, and I have had it bumping the bottom in 19 feet of water. A very violent-actioned lure. You can feel vibrations down the rod during the retrieve.

Heddon Glo Head Hunter — This is a new lure in the UK and I only mention it because of the luminous colours which can show up at depths of 9 feet. I have not used the lure but it's worth mentioning that if exposed to a light for a few seconds they glow in the dark!

Heddon Deep Diving River Runt — plastic. Large metal diving vane. Probably the deepest working of any lure. Dives to 20 feet depending on speed of retrieve (manufacturer's claim). Violent wiggle-action with rattle.

Helin Swimmer Spoon — 3½″ 1oz size, metal. Claimed to be the world's only swimming spoon. This imaginative lure is without a shadow of doubt the best spoon-type lure I have ever used. Its aqua-planing effect actually allows the spoon to be fished at the required depth without sinking beyond the required depth. I once had seven pike in eleven casts fishing the lure about 10 feet deep in eighteen feet of water. The colour of the lure was fluorescent red, a particular favourite.

Helin Flat Fish — 6″ 3oz, wood. This big lure is the most violent-actioned lure I have ever used. The rod tip is thumping all the time the lure is being retrieved. This lure has not been particularly successful for myself but friends have taken good fish on it.

Mepps No. 5 Spinner/Gold Ondex No. 5 — Silver with red tag. These two spinners are about the best of the spinning type of lures I have ever used. Available from most tackle shops.

That then is a very brief description of lures that have been particularly successful for myself. I make no excuses for 95% of them being of USA origin—I simply find them the best. Of course there are hundreds more but I do not think it proper to list any I have not used, or any lure that I have not had at least three pike on!

All the big fishing tackle companies usually stock a range of lures. Abu lures are excellent. Gudebrod lures have a claim to fame with the Sniper (now no longer made, I beleive). This list is endless.

There are always arguments about light conditions and the colour of lures. Personally if I had to choose just four colours they would be white, with red head, perch or pike scale, yellow and black.

PLUG PATERNOSTER

BALL
BEARING
REEL LINE   SWIVEL   TRACE

BOMB

A USEFUL RIG FOR GETTING A PLUG DOWN DEEP AND FISHING IT ALONG AT A SET DEPTH ABOVE A SNAG FREE RIVER OR LAKE BED.

8 Hotspots, Feeding Periods & Prebaiting

During my travels around the country I meet a wide variety of pike anglers, many of whom catch plenty of good fish each season. Most of the top pike men seem to be nothing special when it comes to methods and the quality of their tackle. What then makes them so deadly effective at catching pike? Is it just luck? I think one has to be realistic and accept that many good pike anglers do possess a certain amount of the 'GB' or 'jam' factor, unfortunately the amount available to even the most fortunate angler is not enough to keep the pike flowing in forever. Something else is required and it is not matched carbon rods and a one piece nylon fishing suit! What is required is an understanding of the two most important facets of pike behaviour, hotspots and feeding periods. Without an understanding of these two factors you will still catch pike and probably some big ones. However, for the time put in, your efforts will be rewarded with comparatively few fish, simply because you will be fishing long hours in possibly the wrong areas.

Hotspots are not difficult to define and my definition comes very close to the Barrie Rickards' original. A hotspot is a small area within a water, where medium and large sized pike can be caught regularly. Hotspots are permanent in nature, exist throughout much of the year and can be relied on to produce big pike for a long period providing they are not subjected to intensive fishing pressure. The area around is notable for its lack of big pike, or seeming lack of them. Hotspots are features of large waters, generally very big stillwaters, long rivers and drains, and can only exist when the pike population of a water is fairly large. Waters with very low densities of big pike seldom have hotspots. The reason for the hotspot phenomena are fairly obvious. Firstly it must be accepted that pike move about a lot and tend to hunt over a large area. Pike therefore move into hotspots and out again. The period spent in the hotspot is very dependent on the amount of angling pressure applied to that area. Pike generally move away once captured, though they will often return at a later date. Therefore the more big pike present in a water, the more big pike will be present in the hotspot, and the greater the angling pressure the greater the number of big pike which move out.

It is possible by intensive fishing to disperse all the pike in a hotspot, the pike learning to avoid the area. Therefore hotspot fishing is very much a case of keeping the swim secret and fishing it lightly throughout the season. In this way a lot of big pike can be caught over a season. One swim I once fished produced 30-odd doubles, including 5 twenty pounders, during the period November to March. I managed this by keeping quiet about the swim and fishing it regularly for short periods.

Accepting that a certain style of fishing pays dividends when hotspot fishing, we ought to answer the question, 'What makes a hotspot?' Though it is not essential to know why one swim is a hotspot and another a 'duffspot', it helps to understand the possible reasons for their existence, when it comes to locating them. Though most hotspots defy an instant explanation, as time goes by it usually becomes evident that food fish are not far away. Some of the best hotspots of my experience have been relatively near to where large shoals of bream are regularly seen or caught. The pike hotspot is not slap bang in the middle of the bream shoal's favourite area, but usually not more than 500 yards away. Other prey fish often live in the same area, so it is obvious that the pike have all they need in the way of food, within reasonable swimming range. The pike in hotspots tend to feed for short periods and this may entail hunting out of the hotspot or simply feeding on anything daft enough to be in the area at the time.

Some hotspots defy any reasonable explanation and the two hotspots which were to be found on Hornsea Mere are such examples. Though I had 20 doubles from one of them I never felt that I understood why I caught in such small areas. Ray Webb thought that the pike had moved into the sanctuary to avoid the immense amount of boat traffic on the water and this may well have been true, but it still does not answer the question: 'Why were the hotspots in the sanctuaries so small?' If the pike had moved out of the main part of the mere to escape the tumult, one would expect that any long cast into the reserves would produce the pike. This was not the case and I suppose the answer will never come to light unless I don swimming gear. The important thing to remember is to accept that hotspots exist even if you do not know why!

Hotspot fishing changes pike fishing results beyond recognition. With a good hotspot at one's fingertips it is possible to average a double figure pike every trip, which is very good going. Sometimes it will be possible to catch large numbers of big pike — although the most I have had from a hotspot was 5 doubles, other pike anglers have had twice as many as this in one session. The average size of the pike will usually be high and this reminds me of my last really good day on one of the Relief Channel's best hotspots. The hotspot was first 'discovered' by local anglers, but it was not until the Cambridge Pike Anglers arrived on the scene that the true significance was realised. As usual, I was late on the scene and only realised in 1970 on publication of 'Fishing for Big Pike' what it was all about.

In September of 1974 I spent some time fishing this particular hotspot with initially very little to show for my efforts. Each trip was rewarded with the odd small pike, zander or good-sized eel—hardly what one expects from a hotspot. Still, being persistent types and with few other ideas at the time, Andrew Mack and I decided to give it another bash. The two of us managed to squeeze into the hotspot and were greeted shortly after our arrival by the sight of a pike swirling about 30 yards out in the gentle swell. This was something we had not seen in a long time so obviously we were cheered by the sight. I quickly cast out four different baits, offering the usual variety of live and dead-baits. A short while later Hugh Reynolds and his brother Dick turned up. Hugh fished opposite us on the other bank while Dick fished for bream further downstream. At about 8 am my float legered half herring decided to make for the far bank and I expected yet another eel run. I was pleased to note on winding down that it was no such thing! After a typically spirited fight and a careful netting by the sedges I had the first fish of the day on the bank. It weighed 14lb 1oz and was a typical channel fish, solid and muscular. Quickly returned, I replaced the herring tail with a head. A short while later a large rudd livebait float paternostered about 20 yards out was taken and another hard fight produced an 18 pounder. The wind was now a stiff breeze blowing straight into our bank, but it did not really matter as the pike appeared to be feeding close to our bank. Hugh on the other bank was having a frustrating time with the eels and it seemed as if the pike were keeping the nuisance fish out of the area we were fishing. Later still, and I was stuck into a heavier fish which had picked up the herring head. This was to be my first twenty to a head end bait and proved to be a 42 inch fish weighing 22¼lb. After that fish things went very quiet, Andrew having had only an eight pounder. At about 11 am a float legered dead rudd was finally taken and very quickly I had the fish, which looked like a twenty pounder, on the surface. It opened its large mouth and swirled violently on the surface. After a couple of runs up and down the sedges we had it in the net. I don't think that I have had any more anxious moments than when that fish swirled on the surface. The pike of this particular hotspot were notorious for fighting hard and running into the sedges and then breaking free, so to get that fish in the net took a lot of breath holding! She weighed 23¾lb and remains till this day my best ever channel pike.

This solid fish weighed 18 pounds and was the third biggest in a 4 fish hotspot catch.

Subsequent examination of the photographs showed this fish to be the same fish as a 22½ pounder caught a mile further downstream the year before. I am fairly certain also that this fish came out again in 1978 when Hugh Reynolds caught it at 28½lb and Dave Litton had it at an even larger size, 31lb 2oz.

The next day I blanked while Andrew took a 21 pounder. By any standards an excellent two days' fishing, but for this particular hotspot, not that unusual. Sadly the decline of the Relief Channel resulted in the demise of that hotspot, but time moves on and new hotspots were found and so pike fishing went on. The beauty of hotspots on really big waters such as the Relief Channel is that the pike are concentrated in a limited area. If one tried to locate pike which were thinly spread about the fishery, one's results would probably be poor; however, because the pike are not scattered but are concentrated in the one area most of the time, big hauls are on the cards. Unfortunately this also implies that the rest of the fishery will be even more sparsely populated! The danger of hotspots is that pike killers can effectively ruin a whole water without ever having fished the rest of it. This is another good reason to keep very very quiet about such swims. Once in a while hotspots get discovered by match anglers or 'noddy' pike anglers. This can be very bad news, unless they fail to appreciate the significance of the swim. If you get onto such a swim by whatever means, i.e. seeing someone catch a pike and kill or mishandle it, then I believe that you are fully justified in fishing the swim, to the exclusion of less thoughtful anglers. The same does not apply to other serious pike anglers; a loose code of conduct needs to be followed in order to avoid falling out. If I am fishing a new water with friends and I discover a really good swim, I expect to be able to fish it another couple of times without them having fished it. After that it is a free-for-all. Similarly I restrain myself when a mate has a good catch in a certain swim, unless he makes it clear that he does not mind me having a go.

Hopefully I have made clear what exactly a hotspot is and the reader must by now realise that hotspots are fairly rare. Fortunately there are other phenomena which also involve concentrations of pike, which can be located and caught. These are 'transient hotspots' and 'holding areas'. Transient hotspots are areas where food fish are very numerous, the area surrounding the food fish being relatively devoid of them. They exist for short periods, generally in specific climatic conditions or at certain times of the year. Classic transient hotspots are areas of deep water where fry congregate during the winter. Bridges may also attract large numbers of small fish at various times of the year. If the prey fish remain in these certain areas for any length of time, then pike very quickly home in on these concentrations. Eventually floods or predation pressure from the pike may disperse these concentrations. Most of the transient hotspots I have fished have been good for pike for 2 to 6 weeks. The number of good pike landed depends again on the size of the water and, of course, the pike stocks, but particularly on reservoirs some really huge hauls of big pike have been made. Finding transient hotspots is fairly easy for one has only to keep one's eyes open for signs of prey fish activity and pike swirling. Any area which holds an unusually high concentration of prey fish for any reason, for any lenth of time, should be investigated. I am a great believer in driving round looking at waters, particularly on really bad days when I'm not catching much. Every so often I obtain a clue and sometimes the follow-up produces some good pike. I remember one November keeping my eye on one particular swim on the Relief Channel. Fry were present on several visits over a couple of weeks so I decided to try it. The result was several good pike up to 22½ pounds, ample reward for a little observation.

Holding areas are a totally different kettle of fish, if you'll pardon the expression. Holding areas are in some ways like hotspots, but they are always of a very limited duration and they are also very widespread and quite common on most waters. They are not permanent features and though they can exist in the same spot for several years they frequently change position. Holding areas are particular swims where pike congregate for short periods. Such favoured swims are stopping off points or even specific feeding areas, where pike may be found in between movements. Pike may of course be captured anywhere on most waters, but there is a greater chance of catching pike in these areas rather than when they are in transit between them. Holding areas seldom contain very many fish and tend to empty and fill independent of angling pressure, except that really hard fishing will tend to see them more often empty than full of pike. Locating holding areas is usually by fishing all over a water and learning to identify specific areas from which pike are caught. There are few clues to guide us and hard work is the only answer.

Holding areas seldom produce more than 4 or 5 doubles in a season and frequently fail to re-establish themselves the same season. Sometimes a holding area will produce again the same season, but frequently one has to wait a lot longer for the pike to reappear. That the pike move out of the holding areas to others, often some distance away, has been proved by the tagging or identification of specific pike. Provided one knows a water really well it is quite common to catch the same pike in several different holding areas during a season. The problem of holding areas moving defies an immediate explanation, though I feel sure that the underwater features, however small, can have a considerable bearing on whether or not a holding area stays put. A couple of years ago the dredgers worked along the whole Middle Level drain. The result was that most of the holding areas were lost and pike started to turn up virtually anywhere. Probably in the next few years the bed will stabilise and new holding areas will appear. The fact that holding areas can move makes fishing more interesting, but also creates a fatal trap which can easily be fallen into. Up until a few years ago I used to fish a holding area which I called the matching pairs swim. Most times when I fished it, I caught a good fish and my companion had a similar fish. The best day produced a 19.10 and a 18.10 to myself and Bruno Broughton. However, one year I was fishing with Ian Reeve, with Ian a suitable distance from where I thought the fish were. I proved to have made a big mistake, for the holding area had moved about 200 yards and Ian subsequently thrashed me with a good catch of pike. The new holding area produced quite a few good fish including my old friend the 19.10 to Dave Phillips at just over 23 pounds. It remained in its new position for several years while the old one never fished again. The winter floods may have moved the bed, who knows? Whatever the reason, it pays to avoid getting too set in one's ways, for while hotspots stay in one spot, holding areas do not, and realising this is a vital step towards putting more big pike on the bank.

The art of fishing holding areas is to know when to move and when to stay put. If the feeding times of the pike differ (from past experience) from holding area to holding area, then it is possible to cover several in a day and thereby increase the number of pike caught. Any such increase in numbers of pike caught should favour the capture of more big pike, a simple case of proportion. However should the pike in a holding area show erratic feeding periods, then you have to consider fishing the swim for a much longer period. It is unfortunately quite easy to move out of a seemingly empty swim before they come on feed. This is usually brought home vividly by another angler moving in and catching a load of fish! Still, we all make mistakes.

In a rather subtle manner we appear to have started to consider the other really important factor in pike fishing: feeding periods. An understanding of feeding periods will put the pike angler streets ahead of his contemporaries as I hope to show! That pike have feeding periods has been known for some years now. Many writers have noted that pike tend to feed at certain times. These feeding times vary from year to year, from water to water, and with the passing months. However on many waters the changes in feeding periods are predictable and recur regularly each season. The pike angler seeks to identify feeding periods and then gear his fishing effort accordingly. Initially this requires fishing all day long in a number of different swims. If you are fishing a particular water with friends, the feeding periods can be identified very quickly. Remembering that feeding periods tend to change with the months, it is essential to make one's observations over the whole season.

The majority of pike on most waters feed mostly during the morning. This is certainly true of nearly all the waters I fish during the autumn. From September to November I would say without hesitation that one hour after dawn to mid morning is the time to catch big pike. At this time of year late morning, afternoon and evening feeding periods are fairly rare. As we approach winter, feeding periods invariably get later in the morning and earlier in the afternoon, until in December and January, late morning to early afternoon can be the best time. In winter dawn and dusk are so often a waste of time I am often tempted not to get up so early or stay so late. However if it is a nice day I will often spend a whole day fishing, simply because I enjoy being there. Of course most of the time I gain nothing in the way of pike from the exercise, but that's pike fishing for you!

Learning when the pike feed on a particular water should increase the pike angler's capture rate. If a number of waters exist in one area and some have different feeding periods, then moving from one to the other can increase catches enormously. Of particular importance is the fact that the angler should end up fishing each water at the most productive times, thus saving a lot of wasted time. The pike on some waters can be so predictable that the arrival of the pike anglers can be predicted. One water I know has two feeding periods, from one to two in the afternoon and the other around four p.m. Usually at about half eleven the regulars arrive after having fished other waters. Those who fish the water all day get nothing extra and just waste their time.

Feeding periods can, on some waters, be very short and sharp, leading to the ridiculous situation of having two runs at once. This happened several times on Hornsea Mere always, it seemed, as the massive starling flocks had started to circle overhead. When this happens I strike one fish, guess its weight and if it is small I strike the other rod. I then wind in whichever one feels heaviest. The bale arm on the other rod is then released allowing the fish to swim off if it so wishes. These short sharp feeding periods were the cause of my eventual demise on Hornsea, for I seemed to be staying out on the mere later and later to get that last feeding period. Eventually they banned me! Still fished it though, but this time with a false beard and dark glasses, but that is another story! When pike are feeding for very short periods it pays to have a spare rod set up so that the one in action can be replaced as soon as possible. Also, all traces should be at hand in case a quick change is required — it is no use fiddling about making traces while the pike are on the feed. On some waters different swims produce pike at different times and this may be due to the movement of pike around the water. Here again, moving swims at the right time can increase your catches.

One of the biggest enigmas to confront the pike angler is night-feeding pike. A number of well known anglers have caught pike during the night while fishing for other species, and here and there round the country some pike anglers have actually done quite well at night. I have also fished at night for pike, when sport has been poor during the day. Though I have had a couple of doubles up to 18½lb I have not really been over-impressed by the results on my waters. The nights which have proved of limited success have been mild winter nights with cloud cover, though eel activity even in November has been enough to drive you mad! Frosty nights have been a waste of time and also very cold, minus 7°C being my night fishing record low. Such low temperatures lead to freezing rod rings and solid water, so it is probably a waste of

My second biggest gravel pit pike, 26.00. This fish was in superb condition (only 40½″ Long) and fell for a float legered sardine, March 1982.

time to persist in such extreme conditions. One thing is certain, and that is that big pike hunt in very shallow water at night, an 18½lb gravel pit pike having crept right next to my livebait bucket, in very shallow water, before I disturbed it with a deadbait and two trebles! The idea of tethering an attractant like a bin of livebaits close to a bait appeals to me, and I will be trying it next season. The vibrations which come from a bin of livebaits ought to attract any feeding pike, day or night, but night time is, I feel, the best time to be able to get the pike in close. One thing is certain regarding night fishing for pike, on many waters it is a waste of time, although it is always worth giving it a try just to find out. Night-caught pike could give you an edge on really hard fished waters and no-one would ever know you were catching.

The concluding part of this chapter deals with one aspect of pike fishing which is related to hotspots, and this is prebaiting. Over the years the subject of prebaiting has been given several mentions and the methods used have ranged from scattering a few free offerings around, to the employment of bags full of rubby dubby. My contribution to this somewhat underrated method of getting pike into a swim mainly concerns heavy prebaiting with dead fish. The objective has been two-fold:

Returning a hotspot pike. Exactly 26 pounds, measuring 40½ inches, my 30th double from the hotspot in 4½ months.

one, to attract and hold big pike in a hotspot or holding area, two, to make those pike put on weight! After putting the method into operation on a number of gravel pits, with some success on each, I can hopefully give the reader some indication of how to set about prebaiting in a worthwhile manner. Firstly, the water selected must be a good deadbait water. If the pike do not regularly fall to deadbaits, forget it. Secondly, you have to pick a spot the big pike prefer to be in, i.e. a hotspot or a holding area. Presumably the angler has fished the water before and has some idea of the pike stocks. Bait should be introduced after each session. The amount put in depends on how many pike you think are present, the water temperature, and when you next intend to fish the swim. I generally in winter try and throw a couple of pounds of dead fish into the swim and then leave it for about three days. This gives the pike time to pick the baits up and hopefully keep them in the area for long enough so that I can have a crack at them. If the number of pike caught increases I increase the amount of bait thrown in. If the fishing falls off I reduce the amount. The important thing to try and aim for is a few dead-baits always in the swim. In this manner passing pike are likely to be held in the swim for longer periods giving the angler ample opportunity to catch them.

The type of baits you throw in does not matter. I dispose of all my old baits, be they freshwater or sea fish baits, by cutting them up into small bits (this punctures the swim bladder and also makes the pike hunt for its food) and then scattering them around the swim. Some pike really hog themselves on the baits and I have caught some really fat pike after heavy prebaiting including a 40½ inch 26 pounder! Provided one continues to prebait regularly throughout the winter the extra food must help the pike to put on weight and in so doing improve your tally of big pike. Such situations exist for many other fish species, particularly carp. My observations made while prebaiting one swim suggest that in time all the pike in a water can pass through one swim. I noticed this after having released a couple of pike into the pit I was fishing. These characteristically marked fish were released at the other end of the large pit, but were soon caught a few weeks later in the prebaited swim. So in some cases, once a good swim has been located it might be a waste of time trying elsewhere. The biggest problem I have noticed while pre-baiting is that certain fish stay in the swim and refuse to leave it. This means that they get caught almost every trip. I have no method of avoiding such fish, so I suppose one has to enjoy it. Every so often one gets a surprise and I remember saying to Trevor Moss one day, 'I reckon I have caught every big pike in this pit'. He laughed and said I was barmy. A few minutes later the sardine float slid away and shortly afterwards a superb 26 pounder was on the bank. I have no objection to being proved wrong, once in a while! That fish had never been out before, but the next fish, a 17 pounder, was an old friend of many past captures. I am still very much in the experimental stage with prebaiting, but now know that it has a lot of potential. I also know that old ideas such as pike swallowing deadbaits without moving off is a fallacy. The only way to convince yourself that prebaiting is good for your results and also the pike, is to try it yourself.

9 Different Waters & Horses for Courses

It is all very well to have a good working knowledge of all the methods which can be used to catch pike, and also all the baits one could wish for, provided you can locate the pike in the fishery you choose to frequent. Because pike are found in virtually all types of rivers, drains and stillwaters, the pike angler must expect a variety of problems to surmount. Each type of water has its characteristic features which, once identified, can aid the angler in his efforts to extract some good pike. Though the basic pike fishing methods can be applied to nearly all the different types of waters, there are modifications and adaptations which will make the standard approach more suitable for a perhaps more specialised type of water. Important factors such as location of the pike can be very different on gravel pits compared with rivers, small lakes and big lochs. Many pike anglers will not branch out and explore new types of waters. These anglers prefer to get to know in detail certain types of waters. They may even become specialists in fishing certain types of water. However the more ambitious angler is also more likely to catch more and bigger pike in the long run, even though early efforts may meet with failure. A wider choice of waters increases the opportunity for coping with adverse weather conditions, and also enables the angler to fish waters which are 'on song' rather than persisting with a dour water until a breakthrough occurs. I think it was Martin Gay who placed great store on the fact that different waters, even in close proximity to each other can fish well or badly at different times. Having a wide choice of waters and knowing when to fish each one is the real secret of successful pike fishing. Fancy tackle and baits cannot be used to any great advantage on pike which do not want to know!

Much as I would like to, I cannot tell you here what turns your particular water on or off. Fisheries are so varied that generalisations are always spoiled by pike which do not believe in generalisations. What I can do is show how I would tackle each of the varied types of water, note the most productive conditions and also tell a story or two about what happened when I got everything right. Here and there I might also tell about when I got things wrong. This to me is the real challenge of pike fishing. If you can figure out where, when, and how to catch the pike on a variety of waters and spend more time catching fish, than trying to catch them, then you have achieved something. If at a later date you manage to cut the wasted time down further, then you really are making progress. But first of all, before you even get the rods out, you have to find a water with some good pike in! The first thing to do is think positively — nearly all waters can produce big pike. The ones to check out first are the larger waters of over 2 acres, which have preferably not been fished extensively. Such waters are rare in some areas, and in this case you have to resort to the local or national fishing papers or perhaps your local grapevine. No, I'm not suggesting you start bottling home-made wine, I am suggesting that the best way to get to know about good pike waters is to mix with other pike anglers or perhaps join a specimen group. Do not expect people to put things on a plate for you; in specimen groups, in particular, it pays to contribute as much as you get out of the group. What this usually amounts to is a swop of, say, a tench water for a pike water or something like that. A less desirable approach is to visit waters on Saturday and Sunday and look for pike anglers. If there are a lot fishing a water, it might be a good water. However I would not personally advise this approach, one, because other pike anglers won't love you for it and two, if there are other pike anglers fishing, you are less likely to do well.

The best approach is to go exploring on your own or as a group and investigate the potential of lightly fished waters. Provided pike killing has not been the norm, you should eventually produce the goods. The ultimate size of the pike you catch depends on your luck when it comes to choosing waters, but it is very true that the first anglers really to get to grips with a water usually reap the greatest rewards.

Each type of water is dealt with in turn and here and there I have asked friends, some well known in pike fishing circles, others less well known, to relate exceptional days or periods in their fishing which really proved to be notable. These 'guest' appearances should provide slightly differing views to my own and also help to fill in where my experience has obviously been less comprehensive. The types of waters considered here are:

a) Fen Drains.
b) Fen Rivers.
c) Fast to moderately paced rivers.
d) Small stillwaters, including ponds and small gravel and sand pits.
e) Gravel pits proper.
f) Lakes, meres and broads.
g) Reservoirs.
h) Lochs and Loughs.
i) Specialised fisheries; Trout waters and artificial pike waters.

a) Fen Drains

Fen type drains are found in a number of areas of England. The most famous fen drains are to be found in West Norfolk and Cambridgeshire; such names as the Middle Level, Sixteen Foot and Twenty Foot are household names to keen pike anglers. In the same area there are also a few drains which are pretentiously called rivers, but which are in fact drains, including the River Delph and Old Bedford River. The huge Great Ouse Relief Channel and the Cut Off Channel are also Fen drains in my opinion. These are obviously just a few of the drains in Norfolk and Cambridgeshire and in Lincolnshire there are a whole lot more. Some really famous names spring to mind, such as Vernatts Drain, the South Forty Foot Drain and Timberland or Martins Delph. Running into the Trent are a number of little-known drains including a once famous water, wiped out by pollution in 1976, the Warping Drain. The Romney Marshes have their drains and Somerset too is richly provided for with the King's Sedgemoor Drain and associated waters. Even in the North West the Crossens river passes for a drain and of course in North Humberside there is the Barmston Drain along with a couple of lesser waters.

Most of these drains were built in the last 400 years as an answer to the problem of marshland and flooding. The main rivers were embanked to prevent flooding and drains were cut through the often peaty soil to carry the excess water to the river. As time went by and the peat shrunk the land around the river fell lower in relation to the river. Windmills, steam engines, diesels and electric pumps have all been used to pump this water out of the drains and into the main river. The peaty land once suitably treated with lime and well aerated soon provided some of the best agricultural land in the country. Not surprisingly the animal and plant life in the drains was equally rich. Other drains are really huge reservoirs. The Relief Channel acts as an 11 mile long space to store excess water from the river Ouse in times of flood. The excess water can then be allowed to flow out by gravity when the tide has ebbed in the tidal river. This avoids the need to install massive pumps to pump water out of the Ouse at high tide. Most of the drains running into the Ouse have large pumps to clear excess water and for most Fenland drains an understanding of drainage methods is useful. Firstly one has to understand that pumping costs money. Diesel pumps use expensive fuel and have to be attended while running. Electric pumps are cheaper to use at off peak times so pumping times are likely to be set. Pumping is seldom if ever for the sake of it. Pumps are either used in anticipation of heavy rain or actually to clear excess water. The rate of flow produced by

Brace of 14 pounders from the Relief Channel in 1978.

different types of pump varies from one drain to another, although generally the bigger pumps have the potential to produce faster flows. Those drains which lack pumps empty by gravitation into the main river, usually at low water. Doors at the other end of the drain close to prevent an influx of river water. Flows in these drains are generally more gentle than in pumped drains.

The depths of the various drains also varies and much depends on the amount of attention received from dredgers. The Middle Level for instance is a deep drain, going down to 16 feet at the St. Germans end. The Old Bedford on the other hand is rather shallow and averages about 4 to 5 feet. Nearly all are very straight, almost featureless and to the uninformed extremely boring to look at, which is of course one of the reasons I love them! A decided lack of holiday makers, kids, tourists and water sports fanatics makes these waters the ideal retreat for the peace-loving pike angler.

From 1963 to 1971 I fished almost exclusively on drain-type fisheries. Obviously I was not alone as some very famous pike anglers were making their names on these waters — members of the Cambridge Pike Club, Barrie and Christine Rickards, Hugh and Dick Reynolds, and Basil Chilvers to name a few, along with visitors Ray Webb, Bill Chillingworth and Bill Giles. During those days anyone who was anyone fished the fens and of course they caught fish. Dick Reynolds caught the biggest pike of the early period, a superb channel fish of 31¼lb, and he's been moaning about it ever since! Later on in history faces like John McAngus and a variety of less desirable ''orrible' Midlanders came on the scene. Nowadays the fishing is not so good, but here and there if you look hard you can still find many of the Fenland anglers of the late sixties plugging away at it. I'm pleased to say that I'm one of them, for though I have tasted better fishing elsewhere, my roots are in the Fens and my first love will probably always be these waters.

Fenland drain pike fishing is very much an autumn and winter pursuit. Though there are exceptions to the rule it is (or was) true to say that pike fishing really gets under way towards the end of October. There may be several reasons for this; perhaps it is to do with the availability of food. During the summer months prey fish are widespread in the typical Fenland fishery and pike must have little difficulty encountering prey fish. However once the first frosts arrive, the weed cover starts to fade away and the prey fish form into much larger shoals. These do not usually stay in one spot all the time and therefore the pike start to hunt more. This hunting and the need to build up additional reserves of fat for egg and milt production is, I believe, one of the stimuli for increased feeding. Though fish feed more and digest prey more rapidly in warm water compared with cooler water, they also waste a lot of energy on what is known as their maintenance requirement. This is simply the amount of food required to keep body and soul together and does not include food used for growth and reproduction. I believe that during the summer, pike on the fen drains feed less than they do in the winter. This sounds strange, but I think there may be an explanation. If a large amount of food is wasted on the maintenance requirement during the warm months, perhaps the pike ceases to feed and goes into a form of hibernation (aestivation, or summer dormancy). It then recommences feeding when water temperatures are lower and conversion of prey to pike tissue is more efficient.

Exceptions to the rule occur and some waters, particularly those suffering a food shortage, as, for example, the Middle Level system and Relief Channel in 1979, produced large pike even during the summer. Food shortages will probably cause big pike to grab any suitable offering and this perhaps accounts for the sporadic increases in the number of big pike falling to legered bread or maggots! In theory one would think that the pike would do better to abandon feeding altogether during the warmer months, but it seems that the urge to eat overrides all other instincts, although despite this most of the pike caught in the summer and autumn are very lean. Known fish from the previous season appear to have shown no growth and it is quite possible that what little growth is possible occurs in the winter. All of this is without much in the way of evidence. Johnson's 1966 study of the Windermere pike did suggest that conversion rates were influenced by seasons, independent of temperature and it may just be possible that the pike in a well balanced water feeds in a very set pattern throughout the year. Russian workers have noticed that predatory fish do the majority of their feeding in spring and autumn, with the summer surprisingly devoid of massive feeding efforts. So there we have it, three more or less interrelated suggestions as to why pike prove very difficult to catch in summer on fen drains. There are of course other possibilities, such as a switch to night feeding, however I have night fished a lot since 1968 and the few summer pike to fall at night were outnumbered by the small number of daytime summer pike.

Similar phenomena also occur on many other types of pike water, but because I first noted this while fishing the fens it has been mentioned here. Because most Fenland pike fishing is a winter or at the earliest an autumn pursuit, few problems are likely to be encountered with rooted vegetation. However don't be fooled into thinking that vegetation will never trouble you. Wait until you've been on the River Delph when it's

Weed is a constant problem in winter. Here the writer prepares to remove yet another string of weed from his line.

in flood. I had just cast out at Welney in the famous bridge pool, while on a backend zander trip last March. I fixed the bobbin on, turned back and saw it drop off. I reeled in to find the line covered in weed. I reckon the water was composed of 50% weed that day. Obviously impossible fishing conditions. Weed, debris and GOS (Great Ouse Snot, as defined by Barrie Rickards) can make fishing impossible during run-offs so one prays for it to be minimised or you fish elsewhere.

Providing the water is running fairly clear it is usually quite easy to present baits during run-offs on Fen drains. During gentle run-offs I like to float leger and fish well over depth so that the bait is fished at the

LAYING ON WITH FLOAT LEGERED DEADBAIT ON A FENLAND DRAIN

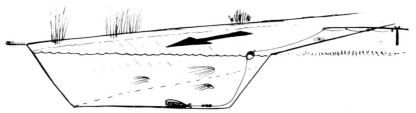

bottom of the shelf, the float resting close to the bank. Livebaits can similarly be fished slightly over depth with the bait just clear of the bottom. It is sensible to hook livebaits head upstream when fishing running water. The bait tends to last a lot longer.

In strong flows I leger deadbaits with up to 2 ounces of lead and fish livebaits on a sunken paternoster with up to 1½ ounces of lead. Weights larger than this make casting awkward and may cause rather more resistance to a taking pike than I would like. Fortunately during run-offs pike are not usually very worried about resistance, though there are exceptions, particularly when the pike are being finicky.

The most important thing to try and do is keep the bait in one place, check it fairly often, at least every hour, for debris and, when fishing close in, be as quiet as possible. Though flow is no real problem provided there is not too much rubbish coming down, the colour of the water can have a considerable influence on your results. Chocolate or tea-brown water is not usually good for Fenland pike, although I have fished on the Relief Channel in these conditions and regularly picked up good pike. Of course such conditions are ideal for zander if your chosen drain happens to have them. Deadbaits appear to be most effective in these conditions, though yet again there are exceptions so it pays to be versatile and to avoid fishing for pike which ought to respond in a certain way! Deadbaits are frequently easier to fish in flowing waters, but this is not really a valid reason for failing to present a livebait properly.

Once you have coped with anything the weather can chuck at you, there still remains the problem of finding the pike. One of the best ways to set to work on a location problem is to do as I did in the early seventies. I decided to explore the Middle Level drain, a relatively unfished drain at the time, which sadly at the present time is not worthy of the big pike seeker's attention. I drew out a map and proceeded to fill in details of all double figure pike caught by myself and friends. Here and there I included fish caught by other anglers (all too often killed). Gradually the gaps were fished and an overall pattern of the fishing evolved. During 1973 there was, as far as I knew, only one genuine hotspot on the Middle Level and quite obviously I fished it regularly. The exploring trips were often conducted with friends, particularly John McAngus during the early days. We had some really good days, simply by picking a stretch and working along it during a day or during a couple of days. I can't remember ever getting a twenty between us, but the information certainly laid the foundation for later successes.

Though no hard and fast rules emerged from fishing the wider Fen drains, odd features proved to be worth a try on many waters. We very

A double in the net.

seldom caught near bridges, unless they were long since demolished. Obvious features such as bends and narrow or wide bits were frequently disappointing — often the pike would be about 200 yards away from the features! Points where drains came in were again red herrings, unless you fished a fair distance away from them. Pylons were sometimes very good but nearly always the best pike areas coincided with the best bream areas. This has particular relevance to the Middle Level system and to a lesser extent on the Delph and some of the Lincolnshire drains. Provided one persisted near to a noted bream area, big pike were *always* caught. This seems to be the key on most Fen drains; the hotspots are somewhere near to, or even within, the breams' main patrol and feeding areas. Though the bream are not always in this area, they frequent these areas more often than other areas and this must be of considerable interest to the pike. The only other attraction for fen pike is the concentration of very large shoals of fish round specific features. This used to be a regular feature on the Relief Channel, where sometimes fish of all sizes would gather around the bridges, on others the fish were mainly fry. Either way the pike would eventually find them and we anglers were quick to follow. Downham Market Bridge on the Relief Channel may not look much of a pike holding area today, but in 1968 I can assure you it was the scene of many big pike captures. I myself had three fish in February of that year on float legered whole herring, fished off the bridge. They weighed 21, 14½ and 10lbs, a friend Adam Hurlock adding a 17 pounder for good measure. All that on two herrings, because that was all we could afford in those days! In November of the same year from the same bridge I added a 23 pounder taken on a float fished live dace. That fish took me under the bridge and all over the place before Basil Chilvers netted her for me. Must have been a strong fish because it had Big Bill Chillingworth's trace in its mouth! The bridge fishing episode did not last forever, although in 1973 I did it again off another bridge and this one weighed 22½ pounds. Bridge fishing has several advantages; you can fish your baits free swimming and, if the wind is behind you, drift the baits out a long way. You can also watch your float whizzing along under the surface, always good fun. However it also has disadvantages—apart from probably being illegal—and the problems associated with striking too hard and walking or falling backwards into the road under a lorry. Fish tend to fight differently and it is all too easy to straighten hooks out when a pike thrashes on the surface. Also netting pike singlehanded is also dodgy. You have to walk round the end of the bridge and down to the water. Finally, everyone knows about it when you hook one! I always like the look on passer-by's faces as I hang over the railing with rod bent. One particular village post lady even enquired 'how big that cod was . . .'

Fry also tend to congregate in other areas and in shallow drains they may gravitate towards the deeper water during the first frosts. If this coincides with reductions in water levels due to pumping, it is always worth fishing the lower reaches of a drain. Pike like a good depth of water over their heads and the far end of a drain frequently satisfies this requirement. This form of concentration can lead to some very big catches provided you get there before other equally observant anglers.

Because drain pike tend to move around a lot, as explained earlier, it pays not to be too set in your ways. Hotspots proper are rare on the drains I fish, but holding areas are very common. Once a holding area has produced quite a few pike it is often worth a move to another area, frequently one nearby. Obviously it takes some time to build up an extensive knowledge of the water, but once you have it you can move from spot to spot during a day and sometimes catch pike from different areas. Never persist with a swim once the results have started to decline. It is far better to rest the swim and return at a later date. Always be watchful for the activities of other anglers particularly youngsters or 'noddy' pike anglers. They frequently stumble on holding areas and fail

Settled down for a long stay. Dave Barnes Umbrella Tent and buzzers for extra slow pike fishing.

to realise their significance. Dave Phillips stumbled on one such swim a few years ago when a youngster walked past him and proceeded to spin a bit further along. Dave had had a poor day and was somewhat amazed when the young lad landed a 16 pounder! Later that season and the next Dave took some really good pike from that holding area, including his personal best of 25.14.

Pike sometimes give themselves away in the most spectacular manner, particularly when mad on the feed. A big swirl is sufficient indication to make me move a long way. This happened one October on a classic drain day, frost with flat calm water and bright sunshine. I had caught nothing at all despite moving to a nearby holding area. At about 11 a.m. just as I was giving up all hope I noticed a big swirl about 200 yards upstream from my end rod. With nothing to lose I made the move and within minutes had a nice pike of 15.6 on the bank. The bait was sardine dropped right where the swirl had been! At other times pike will top and tail just like a bream, although unfortunately when they do this you usually blank. Such observations can mark down likely areas and I habitually return to such areas a few weeks later.

Having found the pike there remains only the matter of the weather conditions. Drain pike are rather strange fish in many ways. The most favourable weather conditions for catching them are frequently those you wouldn't rate. On the wide Fen drains the pike are not put off by really cold weather, provided it is not combined with dirty water. In clear water conditions it is almost guaranteed that Fen pike will feed really well even with partial ice cover. The calmer the day the better, and both misty and bright sunny days are ideal. Snow does not seem to do much for the pike or me come to think of it, and the rain is deadly. I have lost count of the number of wasted days in the fens spent getting wet and little else. Early on in the season a good old-fashioned gale can sometimes get the pike going, but in winter it's a killer. The single most important factor governing fen piking seems to be the weather and time of year. Any form of change in the weather, particularly a temperature increase or drop can bring the pike on. A very useful device to have hanging up in the garden is a maximum-minimum thermometer. This will give you some idea of temperature trends during the period leading up to a trip.

The smaller, shallow and narrow Fen drains are a little bit different from the larger ones. Frosts invariably kill sport and the ideal conditions are mild days with some wind. Strong flows tend to set a lot of the previous summer's weed on the move so still water or gentle run-offs are preferred here.

Fen drains, though somewhat in the doldrums recently (at least in East Anglia), have the potential to produce twenty pound pike in reasonable numbers. My last twenty pound pike from the Middle Level drain system nearly turned out to be two twenties in a day. The events leading up to the day in question (December 9th 1979) were rather interesting. I had by pure accident stumbled on a really brilliant holding area during September. Though I had caught as many as 26 zander in a day from the swim and on other days up to three double figure pike, nothing big had materialised. The swim was about 40 yards long with one really good spot next to a small clump of reeds. During the many trips leading up to the day in question, that small area had consistently produced useful fish in hectic early morning feeding spells. Despite the swim being close to a bridge and a main road I had managed to keep it quiet and had the satisfaction of knowing that no-one else was going to cash in on the spot. On that day it dawned rather misty and I was sure that someone else was fishing near the bridge. All through the session I tried to avoid showing a bending rod by keeping the rod low and avoiding splashing. Similarly I avoided using flash photography which meant that the photos turned out badly. As it was, when the mist cleared the mysterious figure proved to be a bush!

At dawn it was zander activity straight away. Four were landed, two small ones and two of 8.02 and 5.12. No pike as yet, so I decided to move one of my baits from the 'hot area'. As I engaged the bale arm and started to wind in I realised that either the smelt had put on weight or something green and spotty had sunk its teeth into my bait! It was a bit late to strike or do anything except keep winding. The fish was motoring well and making those horrible shaking movements which mean one thing usually—a hook right on the end or outside of the mouth. As it came up on the top I could see one point of the semi-barbless treble stuck into the end of the lower jaw. Gingerly I drew it towards the net. Unfortunately she had different ideas and off she went on another head-shaking run. Next time, I thought, and that was the case. Quickly on the scales and back into the drain. At 19.02 it was my best that season from the water. Another smelt was recast to the same position, but an hour later it was the half mackerel which decided to go. I love a good fast deadbait run, when the float cuts through the surface film and drags under. Unfortunately this was one of those which decides to come and sit under your own bank and jiggle about. I hate those sort of runs because I usually miss them. For a change this was not to be the case. Instead the rod bent over and after a short fight I netted a similar-looking fish. However, she was a good bit bigger at 21¼lb. A quick photo on the ground and back she went. That was the lot for that day. I went on to catch several more good pike and zander from that swim, but never a zander over 9½lb or another 20lb pike. It seems to be quite common on Fen drains to catch quantity from some swims with a definite lack of quality. Other areas seldom produce much, but the size of the fish makes up for this. This is worth bearing in mind, as the really big fish do not seem to follow the herd. Perhaps this is why they get big in the first place!

This chapter closes here with a story from a good friend of mine. During the mid seventies Pete Melbourne had a bit of success with the pike on a Lincolnshire drain. In fact it took me a long time to equal his biggest fish of the period, 32.2! Pete tells his story.

32lb 2oz and 27½lb LINCOLNSHIRE DRAIN PIKE

by Pete Melbourne

For two years prior to the winter of 1974 my main effort in the direction of pike had been concentrated on one of the larger of the Lincolnshire drains which feeds into the River Witham. This particular drain had enjoyed the reputation of being a very prolific big pike water during the mid sixties and as a result of this was hammered by all and sundry until, by 1969, catches had fallen to such a disappointing level that most serious pike anglers had moved on to other waters.

During the next three years this drain received little, if any, attention as far as pike were concerned and in the winter of 1972 I decided to spend a few sessions there to determine whether it had regained any of its former glory. To start with I was accompanied by my brother Roger and we were later joined by our good friend Trevor Moss. The results of these sessions were quite encouraging with the landing of one twenty pound fish by Roger plus several large doubles. Naturally we continued to visit the drain and over the next two years took a number of large double-figure fish, topped by one of 24¾ lbs.

The fishing was by no means easy though, and blank sessions were often the order of the day. It was noticeable however that if a double figure fish turned up it was usually a big one, there being a marked lack of fish in the 9 - 15lb bracket. I had no firm idea as to why this was so but for some reason I had the feeling that this water just might be the one to produce a really big pike if I could stick at it long enough. The last two months of the 1973/4 season produced very few fish and I began to wonder if the drain had once again declined to the point where I would be better off moving on to other waters. However a seven month break from pike fishing whilst I went in pursuit of other species rejuvenated my enthusiasm and once again I found myself making plans for a fresh attack on the drain.

The morning of October 9th 1974 found me making my way through the narrow twisting lanes of the fens and as the car jolted down the track leading to the drain the first grey streaks of dawn appeared on the horizon. I clambered over the steep bank which was slippery and treacherous with the torrential rain of the previous two days and was somewhat disappointed to find that the water had risen some four to five feet and become a deep chocolate brown in colour. Normally these conditions are pretty hopeless, but I had found during the previous two years' fishing that a heavy influx of flood water in the River Witham tended to force numbers of pike up the drains, presumably to escape the heavy flow of the main river. I fished two rods as normal, both rigged with 10lb b.s. line, 15lb b.s. traces, each carrying two size eight trebles with the barbs crushed flat. The first rod was baited with a whole mackerel which was float legered whilst the second carried a free roving roach livebait. As the morning wore on a pale, watery sun appeared with a slight westerly breeze which I used to my advantage by allowing it to drift the livebait rig about four feet from the far bank along an underwater ledge formed by the dredging operations of the River Board. The deadbait rig was also kept on the move by casting to the far bank and twitching it back a foot every ten minutes or so in order to increase the chance of a fish locating the bait in such murky water. By moving one rod in front of the other every hour or so I had covered over two hundred yards of water by mid-day but still no sign of a run. The afternoon proved to be just as quiet but the day was pleasant and I was enjoying my first pike session of the winter despite the lack of fish.

By 4 p.m. however I decided to call it a day; if the pike were not interested by this time they were not interested at all. I trudged back towards the car having accepted this as the first of numerous blanks but when I reached my original starting point I had the feeling that I really should make the effort and fish the last two hours into darkness. Anyway I dropped the gear, flicked the deadbait to the far side and settled down to twitch it gradually across the drain. I glanced at my watch, 5 p.m., another half hour and I would head for home. I twitched the bait again and the float jabbed under slightly as I moved it but I put it down to the mackerel dropping into a deeper channel on the bed of the drain; but could it be?—yes, the float sliding away into the depths, a run at last! I gradually tightened down to the fish and upon feeling a solid resistance, drove the hooks home with a firm sideways pull. I immediately realised that this was no small fish as initially there was no movement at all, but a feeling of being attached to an unmoveable dead weight which did not yield an inch as I applied more pressure in an attempt to move the fish from the bottom. Gradually however the fish began heading for the far side of the drain at a steady pace, apparently unaware of my attempts to alter its course with the application of as much sidestrain as I dare. This fish was obviously something of a size which I had never encountered before and I decided to play it with less pressure than I would normally in case of any sudden, unexpected acrobatics. The fish moved steadily up and down the far bank, then headed back to my own side where it came to rest almost under my feet in some six feet of water. I decided to risk raising it to the surface in order to get a good look at it before sod's

Pete Melbourne's 32.02.

law made the hooks drop out and I crouched low against the skyline as I gradually eased the rod back. A diffused yellow-green shape appeared in the murky water and as it neared the surface took on a form and size which my eyes refused to believe. I just crouched there staring; it was immense, great gaping jaws with the trace disappearing inside and huge dog-like eyes which seemed to be fixed directly on me. At this point the fish must have either seen me or realised that it was hooked and made off with a powerful surge which whacked the rod down to the water and had me frantically backwinding in order to keep pace with it. The fish coursed back and forth across the drain occasionally making longer runs up and down the centre channel, but with the drain being no more than thirty feet wide it was a case of following the fish up and down, applying steady pressure, until after fifteen minutes or so I had it swirling in front of me as I slipped the landing net into the water. To my dismay the fish lay flat across the arms of the net with what seemed like a foot or so hanging over either side, but a bit of careful manoeuvring and it folded up into the depths of the mesh; it was mine!

I heaved the net to the bank and lowered it onto a sack, carefully separating the mesh as I did so to prevent the fish rolling itself up. Having removed the hooks I lifted the fish into my canvas weighing sling which hardly seemed big enough for the job and then paused for a while to admire this magnificent creature which good fortune had granted me the privilege of landing. The head was in perfect proportion to the vast body which was criss-crossed with bold, tiger-like markings, the like of which I had never seen on a pike from this drain before, and there was no evidence of the split and ragged fins which are becoming a common sight in some of our hard fished waters. I lifted the fish on the balance and struggled to hold everything steady while I read off the scale. The needle settled at 32lb 2oz, but then I lowered everything to the ground for a few seconds then tried it again just to make sure I was not seeing double. It was correct though, and I am not ashamed to admit that by this time I was shaking like a leaf. I quickly measured the fish, finding the length to be 44″ whilst the girth was 23″, and having removed three scales from the shoulder, slipped it into the sack to rest a while. As I set up my camera on the tripod I looked out across the barren fenland landscape with not another soul in sight and I felt that this was what fishing is all about; the basic need of the angler to be at one with the elements of nature and the ways of the wild creature.

Having attended to the photography I gently lowered this great pike back into its own domain and once again admired those magnificent proportions, until with a dignified wave of that huge tail, as befitted such a fish, she was gone and I was alone again.

After taking such a fish I could not have cared less if I did not catch a single pike for the rest of the winter but I carried on fishing the same drain and although I took several good double figure fish in the following month or two the fishing was very slow, with either no runs at all or if a run did develop the bait would frequently be dropped before any attempt at striking could be made. For this reason I decided to scale down my tackle somewhat, and changed to eight pound line, 10lb b.s. trace and size 10 trebles, in the hope of encouraging more confident takes. For some time conditions for pike fishing on the drains had been hopeless due to unusually low water levels and it seemed that I would not have a fair chance at the pike before the season ended. However, the second week of March 1975 saw the return of torrential rain and while most people bemoaned the weather I happily watched it bucketing down, praying for a heavy flood to push the pike back up the drains.

Work prevented me from fishing until the last day of the season so it was all or nothing as I lobbed two mackerel tail baits to the far side of the drain on the dull, rainy morning of March 14th. The water was three feet above normal but had cleared somewhat and I felt confident that using the lighter gear, plus the fact that the drain had hardly been fished for some weeks, I was in with a good chance of a fish. I had one bait on a freeline rig and at 9 a.m. the indicator slid up to the butt ring and my ensuing strike met with a firm resistance which after a few seconds slackened off as the fish moved smartly across to my side of the drain. I was not quick enough and with the water being fairly clear the fish must have spotted me and took off at great speed, as though it was going all out for the Witham three miles away! This fish was a real fighter, making heavy boring runs shaking its head as it went, attempting to fling the trace free, and by the time I had it over the net my arm was aching and stiff with the constant pressure. With relief I lifted the net to the bank and found the pike to be a typically large-headed drains fish with a very deep girth and an odd light coloured hue to it. I knew it was a twenty but I had not realised just how big until the scales swung round to 27½lbs, a most satisfying reward for a last ditch effort!

Having secured the fish in a sack I drove to the nearest call box and telephoned Trevor Moss who promptly dropped everything, picked up Roger and drove forty-odd miles to witness the pike. Having missed seeing the thirty there was no way they were going to miss this one!

These days this particular drain is not quite the same as it used to be and no really big pike have been taken for some years, but I still spend a few sessions there every winter. The memory of those two big fish is as fresh now as the day I caught them and I have a feeling that one day it will turn up the goods again. I just want to make sure I am there when it does!

Pete Melbourne's 27½.

b) Fenland Rivers

Fenland rivers, though not particularly widespread in England, deserve a special mention, because they can provide superb pike fishing and tend to present different problems when compared with faster moving rivers or drains. My experiences are limited to the large slow moving rivers of Lincolnshire, Norfolk and Cambridgeshire; the most noted rivers in these counties being the Witham, Welland and Great Ouse. Though the Great Ouse is in the doldrums at the moment and not producing many big pike, there is little doubt that it will recover one day and be a water to fish regularly. The Witham has also declined to some extent due to the bream shoals fading away, although the roach revival has allowed it to recover as a pike water, despite the continued killing of big pike by anglers from the Sheffield area. The Welland, frequently the scene of the Angling Times Pike Championships, is a prolific producer of good sized pike and can usually be relied on to produce some good fish, if you fish it regularly. All Fenland rivers are (or were!) noted match fishing waters and this can sometimes make pike fishing difficult. Those such as the Witham are best fished during the week and care has to be taken at weekends not to miss match reservation notices. The nice thing about most Fenland rivers is that roads frequently follow them and access is uniform and easy all along. For those with naughty habits like fishing three or four rods, this is a bit of a nuisance. However you don't get into trouble unless you get caught and this policy generally results in the 'bailiff twitch'!

Most Fen rivers flow slowly all the year round. Sluices control the flow and the rate of run-off is always greater when the water is low in the tidal river. It is also true that most Fen rivers have been straightened and dredged many times over the years. Because of this they tend to be rather uniform waters. Fortunately variations in depth can be found and this may include deeper holes or deeper channels along one bank. These can be of considerable importance to the pike angler and may influence the distribution of the prey fish. One's opening gambit is usually to locate such features and also determine where the prey fish are most often found. Reference to match results, our old standby on the drains, can again be useful.

The average depth of Fen rivers can vary, there being a considerable difference in winter and summer levels on the Witham and Welland in particular. Levels are often kept low in these rivers and depths of greater than six feet can be hard to find. The Great Ouse below Earith, on the other hand, fluctuates very little winter and summer, and is generally 15 to 22 feet deep. On the Ouse the deepest water is found along the lower reaches better known as Ten Mile Bank.

Winter is the normal time for pike fishing on Fen rivers for, like the drains, the rivers seldom fish well before October. If summer fishing was productive the excessive weed growth which lines the margins of waters such as the Welland would tend to make pike fishing difficult, especially in windy weather when the weed tends to drift about. Up until about November most Fen rivers flow slowly and all the conventional pike fishing methods are productive. Once the rains start, as they often do in November, the pike angler starts to encounter problems. Rivers such as the Witham flood very easily and all my experiences suggest that pike fishing then is a waste of time. Apart from the muddy colour, flows are very fast and weed and debris make fishing extremely difficult. I no longer even attempt to fish Fen rivers in these conditions. I go elsewhere! However just as quickly as they flood, Fen rivers fine down much more quickly than drains. At these times prey fish are still sheltering in drain mouths or any other area which provides relief from the flow. Though the river can still be moving like a train, it should be fishable once the brown colour is replaced by green. I try to coincide a trip with a high tide, this tends to reduce the flow to manageable proportions. Baits are generally fished close in, or in drain mouths. Here the pike are often present in numbers and some big bags are possible. Hotspots and holding areas may also exist on a river and once it has fined down these are worth fishing. The pike on each of the three rivers mentioned appear to be fairly catholic in their taste for baits. The Great Ouse is a superb half mackerel water and all sizes of pike fall to this bait. In the past the half mackerel was an incredibly reliable bait for the bigger pike and no doubt in the future this bait will take many more fine Ouse pike. Livebaits and natural baits are also effective on the Ouse, but they have tended to blow hot and cold when I've fished it! On the Witham the livebait is invariably the top bait, but there are days when natural and sea baits do very well. The Welland is a pretty good deadbait water and in my experience sprats, herrings and natural baits are very effective. I've not done very well on livebaits there, but that is probably due to lack of fishing experience there.

On rivers such as the Ouse bait positioning can be critical, and it takes a long time to learn the best swims and where to present the bait. Generally the far bank is a good bet and this is easily reached with any deadbait. I like to float fish wherever possible, but it pays to beware of boats. Dave Phillips came a cropper in this way and while his bait was out of the water I had the only double of the day next to his disabled rod!

On one occasion Barrie Rickards had a huge cruiser, aptly named
Invader, break down in his swim. Dave and I were falling about with
laughter but, gentleman that he is, Barrie sorted out the resulting mess
and continued fishing.

Most Fenland rivers tend to be prolific pike waters and produce a
lot of pike in the 4 to 6 pound range. The Welland and Witham are
particularly like this. On some days it might be necessary to wade
through a dozen such fish to catch a double. All good fun, but worth
taking along some extra bait. On the last day of the 1982 season I was on
the Witham with a handful of rather useless perch livebaits. All were too
big and the result was loads of missed runs. Despite this I landed 6 pike
including three different eleven pounders. I should have had more, but
then you cannot always get it right; six times is enough for a last day
fling!

An insight into Fen river fishing can be gained by reading an
account of a particularly notable day's fishing. Barrie Rickards, who
knows the Ouse inside out, tells all for the first time about his 32lb
record Ouse pike.

Slipping back a plump Ouse 14 pounder.

32lbs, RIVER GREAT OUSE, NOVEMBER 26th, 1976

by Barrie Rickards

Thirty-two pounds, plus an estimated couple of ounces or so; length 47½ inches. For some reason I forgot to take the girth measurement (I'm amazed I remembered to take the length measurement), but we did weigh it more than once, for obvious reasons: at that length it could, with a full belly, have weighed as much as 38 or even 40 pounds. But it didn't and the very centre of the needle hovered a hairsbreadth over the 32lb mark. It certainly wasn't a thin fish, as you can see from the photograph, and it certainly wasn't soft and flabby, but I don't know where the extra 6lbs went! I had the balance checked the next week and it was quite spot on, so no extra poundage there.

This fish is one of the biggest from the Great Ouse River, perhaps the biggest: certainly the longest. By any river fishing standards it is a very big pike. In general, if it's the real giants you want, then lakes and reservoirs, lochs and loughs, are the places to head for. But my Great Ouse thirty pounder is possibly a good example of a big fish caught by a technique and approach especially suited to big rivers in particular, but to rivers in general and it may well be that my approach to the Great Ouse will have wide application and uses elsewhere. For this reason I will account not only for the capture of the thirty, but try to give some idea of my attitudes and approaches.

Until very recently one never had any doubts about the Great Ouse. It had gone on producing good fishing year in and year out, of all species, and the growth rate of its pike for a number of years indicated that several thirty pounders could be present, so choice of water was never really a problem. I simply fished it as the fancy took me, occasionally trying new stretches, often returning to favourite places (not necessarily hotspots which, anyway, are sometimes difficult to pinpoint on rivers and may not exist in the same form as they do on still waters). On November 26th I arrived at dawn at a place where I'd taken twenty pounders previously, where friends had had them up to 24½lbs and where, even if the big ones were off feed, I could expect a bag of 6lb plus fish. I ought to say that my previous thirty pounder (31½lbs in 1972) was caught on November 5th: it's nice to have early winter big ones particularly in November when the rivers are often full of leaves and other decaying plant life.

I received a little disappointment when I arrived at my swim; it was occupied by two Sheffield match anglers on a week's holiday. I did wonder about covering the water from about thirty yards away, but it would have been a churlish decision on my part. Instead I chatted to them for a few minutes, during which time one of them asked, 'Did tha want ter fish here then?' I replied by saying that it didn't matter, I would move upstream of them. The reply was typical of certain friendly northerners: 'Nay lad, we're catching nowt at all, just chuck out in the next spot.' So I did.

I used two rods, one with float legered half mackerel, and one with float paternostered 4 ounce roach livebait. My wife used exactly the same approach, fishing one swim upstream of me. The problem as I saw it was that if the river pulled off at all strongly then my baits could sweep through the Sheffielders' swims in a few seconds. I warned them of the possibility and then took steps to counteract it. On the rod nearest the two match men I used the deadbait, float set some ten feet over depth and, although it wasn't necessary from the point of view of current strength at that time, I put on a ¾ ounce sliding Arlesey bomb. Then I chucked it out perhaps six feet under the far bank. There was a good reason for this. On many big rivers the big pike are not along the edges as common dictum has it, but in the middle or, on waters where only one bank is of common human access, some distance over the halfway mark. By casting just under the far bank the bait and lead would come to rest at the top of the slope into deeper water, or on the slope itself. Once everything was settled down, and the current strength tested, I could ease the bait slowly down the far slope and then very slowly towards the middle, taking a couple of hours over this procedure. It had the added advantage that if a sudden upsurge of current occurred my gear would be swept *beyond* the match anglers and I could walk my rod over their heads without otherwise disturbing them.

In fact, those two hours didn't happen! After perhaps forty-five minutes, the float shot away downstream, travelling just under the far bank; without following it I hooked into a solid fish which eventually came in with the mackerel hanging in its scissors, neatly hooked. That went 8¾lbs, a short fat fish. The mild commotion drew a head over the willow herb of the next swim, a thumbs up sign, a grin, but no real interest in a mere pike. As the mackerel tail was still in one piece, still firmly tied on, I chucked it out again into the same spot, tightened up a little and sat back to wait. Meanwhile my livebait rod worked away slowly and steadily, just inside halfway across, but otherwise gave no signs of abnormal movement. On this latter rod I had the bait down about eighteen inches off the bottom in quite deep water, but with a seven foot paternoster link terminating in a ¾ ounce lead. Fished this way they work slowly and steadily, over quite an area, and yet are firmly anchored. The result is that you fish exactly where you want to fish and yet the bait has quite a 'drawing' area. A long paternoster link fished like this would not work for some species, but with roach it works extremely well. Another general point about paternostered livebaiting is that the bait remains perfectly fresh and active unless taken by a pike. I sat back in the knowledge that if the bait wasn't taken I could take it off the (small hook) snap tackle and return it to the water with little more in the way of damage than that caused by the original capture, a point not always realised by anglers who think of livebaiting as it was in the distant past.

I was vaguely pondering these thoughts when the deadbait rod shot off again in a quite identical run to the previous one. The fish gave a spectacular acount of itself, was similarly scissors hooked, and this time weighed 9¾lbs. It was only a short while after I'd returned the fish (to the mock horror of the match men) that I heard the silver paper slip off the butt of the livebait rod (where it held the line against the corks) and saw that the float had dropped out of sight. The fish ran slowly upstream and after it had run steadily for some five yards I wound down and hit it hard. It would in fact have been quite close to Christine's deadbait line, but would have run underneath it. This was clearly a better fish and gave some lively runs before being netted: 12lbs exactly. The match men were now enjoying the proceedings and probably realised that once the pike went off the feed the roach would come on.

So far one of those good days, with good fish, and nothing going wrong. About an hour later exactly the same thing happened: the silver paper rustled off the corks, hung momentarily on the line, which peeled slowly through it, and then fell to the grass. The float was gone and the fish moving steadily upstream. As the bait was slightly larger I allowed it to go under the deadbait line and then struck hard and low to my left. The rod was almost wrenched out of my hands, the handle spun back-wards with rapidity and the pike shot out across the middle, staying deep. It was clearly heavy and made several runs of great power, prob-ably never once coming up more than a foot off the bottom. Eventually it did come up a little, fortunately missed the deadbait line, stopped fighting for a few moments, and then started aquabatics close in to the reed beds. It was so obviously a big twenty that once it hit the surface I hustled it over the net and slid it up the bank. No real problem at all. As with the others it was hooked firmly in the scissors and, like the previous fish, the livebait had gone. By now the two matchmen arrived, stood in considerable awe, and watched it unhooked. I was excited, naturally,

Barrie Rickards with his superb Ouse record pike of 32 pounds.

because it was clearly a thirty pounder, the only question being how many pounds (not ounces) it was over that weight. But never have I seen two other anglers so excited as the two Sheffield anglers. For a while they would come no nearer than three or four yards, and with the expanse of bank available were able to walk all round the fish without actually going near it! Eventually they plucked up courage when they saw that it handled easily, and they even took some pictures for me.

The story doesn't end there. I'd forgotten my cameras (a frequent occurrence) so Christine had to drive to Cambridge to get them whilst I kept the fish in the net. She was back in half an hour or so and we took some on our cameras. The match anglers were still smiling when the fish was returned; they didn't stop smiling for the rest of the day. I've never seen a couple of chaps so pleased at seeing a big fish. But it was more than a year before I heard from them again. On the way home they'd crashed their car and finished up in hospital for six months. It was only when sorting out their tackle boxes on beginning fishing again that they found their camera, got the film developed and sent me a packet of prints. It arrived through the post like one of the many surprise packages that go to make up angling, and it drew the curtain upon a memorable day.

c) Rivers

In this section I intend to look at river pike fishing and having already dealt with the Fenland rivers, this leaves the field clear to consider the faster moving ones. My experience of river pike fishing is fairly varied, but obviously with the variety of rivers up and down the country I cannot hope to have fished them all. My river fishing has been conducted on the River Hull and River Ure in North Humberside and Yorkshire, various Norfolk rivers such as the Bure, Wissey, Nar and Babbingley and more recently on the River Trent. River fishing is usually very interesting fishing, though few rivers can match stillwaters for the sheer size of pike caught. The average size can still be very high and river fishing is frequently easy fishing compared with most other types of pike water.

Because river pike tend to be very active, hunting widely and also having to counter the force of the current, they tend to be opportunists and will nobble a bait at all sorts of times of the day and year. Against this advantage, one has to consider the effect of weed growth and weed cutting, floodwater and fast flows. Rivers have to be fished when conditions are good as the pike are usually turned off quite easily by less than ideal conditions. Coloured water, particularly when it is a muddy colour, kills all the clear rivers I have tried. Similarly, when a lot of weed is on the move, the pike seldom seem to want to know. The best conditions I have noted on most rivers consists of clear water at normal winter level, with no muck coming down. Frequently you get this several days after the river has been in flood. The water may appear slightly green, but in reality it will be fairly clear. The water temperature can be very low, but pike can still be caught. Bright sunshine is a good sign and I positively relish fishing any river after a frost. Not all rivers fish to this pattern. Broadland's River Bure still puzzles me and it will be several years before I have really learned enough about this water to be able to predict the pike's likes and dislikes. I have friends who have done well on this river in virtually all conditions, though my limited experience suggests that snow and ice on the water put the pike off. One thing is certain, there are enough pike in the Bure to give the angler a chance of a good fish on even the worst possible day.

Location of pike on rivers depends very much on how much attention the river has had from dredgers. Most rivers have been 'improved' and this can result in rather uniform waters. Given a few years features soon develop. I generally look for any feature on small rivers. This includes deeper lengths, bends, wider lengths and anything at all that breaks the monotony. Few of the rivers I fish have weirs or pools, though I have had the odd pike from lock cuttings. I also like to adopt a semi-mobile approach so that I have fished a fair length of river in the area of a feaure. Pike do not always get caught near the obvious features. One good example of this was a couple of years ago. Kathy and I were out for our annual Christmas morning bash on a local river. The morning was perfect, frosty and soon getting sunny. I picked a silly swim, which had a particularly narrow section of river running through it. Live and deadbaits were positioned at intervals along the river. One smelt deadbait was fished directly in the middle of the narrows. An hour later I had my first run and found that the fish was belting downstream. After a reasonable fight Kathy netted a short solid chunky pike of 20lb 9oz, my best from the river. I didn't get any more good fish, but further upstream David Howard had netted a 17 pounder so it appeared that the pike were feeding fairly well. I do not know if there was something significant about the swim, but one thing was known and that was that few other anglers had fished the swim, and this I feel is important on rivers which are fished a lot. The pike tend to rest in areas which are not flogged and this includes all the likely looking swims mentioned before!

TROTTED LIVE OR DEADBAIT

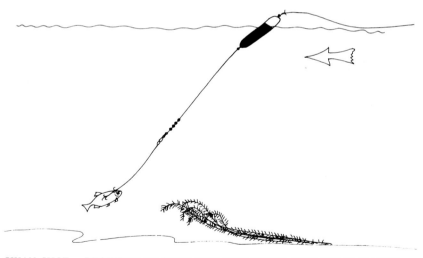

SWAN SHOT — REQUIRED TO KEEP THE BAIT DOWN. THE FLOAT IS BEST FIXED BY A SHOT DIRECTLY UNDER IT, THE BAIT CAN THEN BE CHECKED ON THE TROT WITHOUT GETTING CLOSE TO THE FLOAT.

One feature of the smaller clear rivers is that big pike may be visible to the angler. In pike fishing this is something of a rarity. Because the angler can sometimes see the pike, it also means that the pike can certainly see the angler, and the pike is also bound to hear a clumsy approach. So when fishing such waters it is essential to avoid appearing on the skyline and a quiet approach is the greatest aid to putting a pike on the bank. I prefer to work along the field at the back of the swim (when crops are not present) and creep down to the swim, cast out and then retreat in a similar manner to a position up or downstream of the rods. In this way a bait is left to fish undisturbed. When a run is registered (for this type of fishing drop-off indicators such as those described in the tackle section are very useful), creep to the rod and strike immediately, for river pike seldom mess about. Nearly all the standard methods work really well on rivers. Static live or deadbaiting methods are the mainstay of this type of fishing though when the pike are really 'on' the mobile methods of trotting with a livebait, float trolling with a livebait or deadbait wobbling can really score. In these situations the more water you cover the more pike you catch. The successful river angler will learn to tell whether or not the pike are feeding well or only prepared to take a bait after a long inspection. When the water is really clear it is sometimes possible to present a bait to a pike. Some really interesting fishing can result. I once caught a 16¾ pounder from the River Hull which took my livebait, ejected it and repeatedly swam around it; eventually the simple ploy of pulling the bait away was more than it could stand and it quickly munched the hapless bait. If only the pike angler had many more opportunities to observe his quarry, I am sure the thinking angler would be able to catch a lot of pike.

Though many rivers are rather devoid of obvious features, there are still plenty with some amazing swims. I fish one river which widens out and forms a very big eddy. During periods of low flow the eddy produces only the odd pike. However, once the first floods have swept down the river, thousands of roach fry and much bigger fish gather in the eddy. The pike soon follow and sport can be hectic. At times it seems as if the pike can predict adverse weather conditions for before another flood or some really cold weather, tremendous sport can be experienced. It seems as if the prey fish take shelter in the eddy and this drawns the pike out of the main river, with a concentrating effect which leads to the formation of a transient hotspot. My best pike from this swim weighed 20lb 11oz and it could always be relied on when other waters were still in flood. It is having the choice of waters which enables the pike angler to catch in spite of the conditions.

RIVER SWIM OR TRANSIENT HOTSPOT

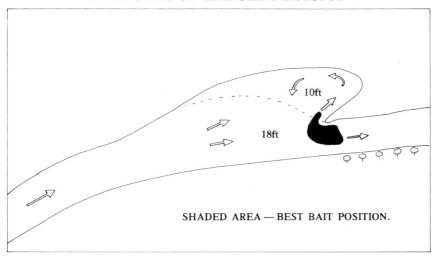

10ft

18ft

SHADED AREA — BEST BAIT POSITION.

On the Broadlands rivers such as the Bure, the pike seem to move about a lot and at certain times of year, particularly towards the back-end, some very big pike are caught from right in amongst the boatyards. At this time of year, youngsters fishing off the jetties have accounted for some surprisingly big fish up to 28 pounds. Whether the pike move off the Broads into the rivers in winter I do not know. It is possible I suppose, but it does not stop anglers catching pike off the Broads themselves even in the winter. On rivers such as the Bure, big pike can avoid being caught for much of the season, simply by chance movements into private Broads or up boat channels. It is this, and the huge supply of food fish which makes the Bure such a good pike water. I have only just got to grips with this water, my best fish going 19.08. It pays not to consider the Bure as typical of Broadland rivers, for there are considerable differences say between the upper Thurne and the Bure. The upper Thurne has produced some big pike in the past season, including fish over 37 pounds. The Thurne is not much to look at up around Somerton, but as you near Martham it widens out. It is a reed-lined river and tends to be very weedy. Even in the winter, beds of marestail are common all the way across the river and this can make bait presentation difficult.

The tidal Waveney at Beccles, on the other hand, tends to be much deeper and runs like a train, depending on the tide. Methods of fishing must obviously vary depending on the type of river you intend to tackle.

My best Lomond pike, a 26 pound 'tailwalker', which took a small paternostered roach livebait during April of 1979.

Smallest fish of a trio of Irish twenties taken in April 1981, 20.06. It took a float legered half trout and fought like a tiger!

The wife with her best small river pike of 13.11.

Where weedbeds are extensive, as on the Thurne, free-swimming float-fished baits, using a greased line, are essential. On the tidal river the paternoster comes much more into its own.

To conclude this chapter I ought to mention the special problems of very big fast moving rivers such as the Trent. In the future there is a very good chance that the Trent will become a first class pike water. It has the food fish—that no-one could argue with. It is also artificially warmed by the many power stations which stand beside it and because of this it never freezes. The most off-putting factor when considering the Trent is the sheer force of the water. Take one look at the Trent and you immediately convince yourself that you cannot fish it in a conventional manner. However, you would be wrong. Provided you do not pick a really swirly or racey swim, a paternoster using a small sunken float and a one ounce bomb will hold a small livebait out nicely. Similarly when legering a one ounce bomb will keep the bait in one place. Obviously it helps to find slack areas if possible. My first trip to one likely-looking slack produced 8 pike to seven pounds, a fair day's sport by any standards. The problem with the Trent is that any amount of rain in the Midlands tends to raise the level and a lot of muck starts to come down. In these conditions it is very difficult to hold out in the main current, so

one tries to find lock cuttings, where pike tend to gather during prolonged periods of high water.

Trent pike seem to like livebaits and natural deadbaits. So far I have
yet to get a fish on a sea fish bait, but it is early days yet. Allen Edwards
tells me that wobbled deadbaits and Mepps spinners have accounted for
fish to 15lbs, so there is obviously more to fishing the Trent than the
methods I tend to use.

My experience of pike fishing on the Trent remains limited, my best
being 9¼lb. This is, I am sure, mainly because of the distractions of
other easier waters in the area. If the Wye, Hampshire Avon, Dorset
Stour and Severn can produce big pike, why not the Trent? After all,
J. W. Martin found it to be a good pike water in the days before it
declined. With the Trent ever-improving, the pike fishing must surely
follow suit.

d) Small stillwaters

One of the most underrated types of pike water is the small still-water. Because of their small size (less than two acres) pike anglers tend to avoid these waters and convince themselves that such waters are incapable of holding any big pike. Unfortunately they are often wrong and the next season some youngster catches a 25lb plus pike! I should know all about this, because I have overlooked such waters in the past. Mind you, I have probably made up for the error of my ways since then. The type of water I am thinking about is the club lake or gravel pit. Small, generally shallow (but not so shallow that the fish cannot survive droughts or freeze-ups) these waters are usually crammed full of fish, fairly coloured and fished every day during the summer. Kids love these waters simply because they can usually catch a fish or two. Some of these waters are even stocked from time to time, so you can see that any pike living there has a very easy life. Every day during the summer damaged fish are released from keepnets and small dead or dying fish must be common. Such waters frequently contain large shoals of skimmer bream so a big pike does not have to look far for its next meal at any time of the year.

The disadvantage of such waters is that they can only support a small head of big pike and obviously if these are killed our interest in the water stops there. Also once such a water is 'blown' to other pike anglers the pressure exerted on the water may reduce the individual's chance of success. The pike in these small waters may be very well fed and conse-quently very difficult to tempt to take a bait. It is certainly true that winter is by far the best time to catch on the really overstocked waters. The last three weeks of the season are a favourite time of mine particu-larly if the weather is unusually mild. Be warned of leaving it too late though. I have fished on some of these waters during the last week of March while they were obviously getting down to spawning. Once this starts it is a wise move to move to a deeper, more extensive, water where water temperatures are likely to be lower. The pike in the larger waters are usually a little later in spawning.

Small waters generally lack really obvious features such as great variations in depth. However, many are often irregular in shape and this can be used to advantage. I always try to fish the part of the pit or lake which enables me to cover as much water as possible. Points which run out into the water are favourite positions and on small waters you can sometimes cover the whole water. particularly when you have it to yourself.

SWIMS ON A SMALL GRAVEL PIT

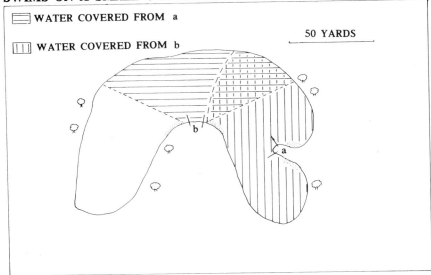

▭ WATER COVERED FROM a

▥ WATER COVERED FROM b

50 YARDS

Big pike are usually few and far between on these waters and because of this it is hard to build up a picture of best swims and the like. In my experience on waters where there are thought to be 1 to 5 doubles, one a season is quite good going! Obviously one does not fish such waters on a regular basis unless you think or know of a very big fish in the water. Even then it is unwise to spend too much time on small waters, because you can be very unlucky, while absolute novices catch the fish you are after! You can be very successful on a small water and still fail to get the big one. I approach these waters as 'quicky trip' waters. I fish them when no-one else is about (no competition!) for short periods on favourable days. Just once in a while I catch a good fish. By playing the field like this it is possible to catch the odd good fish from these small waters while you are concentrating your efforts on much bigger waters.

Weather conditions are important on these small waters and the worst problem is usually freezing, for these waters all too rapidly go 'solid'. The best weather in my experience is mild, very windy weather. Sunshine can be helpful particularly if it is intermittent. Because such small waters are nice and sheltered they make ideal places to fish during winter gales and what's more they usually fish well in these conditions. Frosts and dull calm days are nearly always hopeless.

An incredible fat 20lb (exactly) pike of 35¼ inches.

As far as tactics are concerned, these need not be specialised. Casting distances are very small and physical problems such as undertow are non-existent. Small to medium sized natural deadbaits are frequently very effective on these waters, due probably to the regularity with which pike encounter dead fish on these heavily fished waters. Livebaits usually prove effective float paternostered or legered. It pays on these shallow waters to keep the rod tip up and the line off the water, because a livebait sometimes manages to get up to the surface and this can be disastrous particularly if a pike is following it and hell bent on eating it! I seldom use baits bigger than 4 ounces on these waters, simply because the splash on casting out such large baits seems disproportionately large to the water being fished. Also in small waters you cannot afford to wait too long before you strike due to the proximity of reed beds and snags. This happened to me last season; I had positioned a 6 ounce roach up against a reedbed on a point. Before I knew it a pike had picked the bait up and was heading round the other side of the point. I had to strike too soon and missed the run! If I had been fishing a smaller bait I would have probably hooked that fish.

A few years earlier in December of 1973 on the same water I had been a bit luckier. It was my first trip to the water and I picked the largest area of the pit, positioning a half mackerel and a dead roach in front of me. I had arrived late having been 'pumped off' a nearby drain at 10 a.m., so I had retired here for a little quiet fishing, away from running water and drifting weed. About an hour after casting out I looked up to see my red float racing along the surface towards the mackerel float. With no time to lose I wound down and struck into the fish. Being only 6 feet deep the pike came to the top in seconds, its dorsal cutting the surface. With one slap of its tail it made one half-hearted run before giving up and sliding into the net. In the water it had looked about 13 pounds, but on the bank its tremendous fatness suggested a heavier fish. And so it turned out, for that piggy of a fish measured 35¼ inches and weighed exactly 20 pounds. My fattest pike ever and also my only twenty to be spot on. The fish was a beauty, one of those stripey fish with really vivid markings. A couple of shots with the Instamatic and it was returned. For the next two seasons I struggled on this water to lose one good fish in a sunken tree. A classic example I think of the case for giving up while you are winning!

e) Gravel pits

Gravel pits come in all shapes and sizes, depths, and states of maturity. With the decline of many of our rivers and the silting up of lakes built several hundred years ago, gravel pits have increasingly become the scene of the search for big pike. The fact that gravel pits can be prolific pike waters means that nearly all aspiring big pike catchers will at one time or another have to come to terms with these waters. They are also widespread around the country and this means that most pike anglers will have such waters nearby. Some very big complexes of gravel pits are to be found in particular areas where gravel extraction has been on a large scale. In the south of the country Kent is particularly well endowed with large pits along the River Darenth and around Maidstone. Sussex has a huge complex at Chichester, and along the Thames in Middlesex, Surrey and Berkshire there are many large pits. One of the biggest complexes of them all is in Wiltshire around South Cerney near Cirencester. Oxfordshire is well known for its large pits such as Hardwick and further east we must not forget the many waters in the Lea Valley. Norfolk, Cambridgeshire and Huntingdonshire are less well endowed with really huge pits, but many medium sized waters are available. In Nottinghamshire there is the immense sprawling Attenborough complex and further north around Newark and Lincoln yet more large workings. Gravel pits start to get fewer as one heads north, but there are still some to be found particularly at Brandesburton near Beverly, in North Humberside.

There are many more which I cannot mention or do not know of, but nearly all have produced, or have the potential to produce, big pike. Wherever your chosen gravel pit is, and whatever size, the first job is to get to know the water as well as possible. This may not be a simple task on a 100 acre pit and it is here that a small group of friends can work together to the ultimate benefit of all. My first ploy is to get a boat on the water and make a map using the echo sounder. This requires two of you, one to row or man the outboard, the other to chart the depths. Runs are made back and forth across the pit, noting the depths on a map drawn before you start. Once the pit has been well covered it is simply a matter of joining up all the points of similar depth, to obtain a contour map of the water. I usually make sure the owner or club secretary gets a copy of the map; what you might call in the furtherance of good relations! The features to look for in a gravel pit are many and varied and the features present depend very much on how the pit was excavated. Some pits are nearly uniform in depth, these having been sucked out rather than dug.

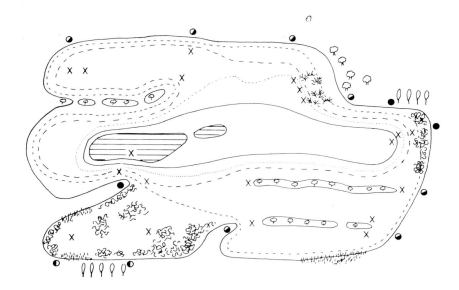

GENERALISED GRAVEL PIT WITH LIKELY SWIMS

KEY

_ _ _ _ _	5ft CONTOUR
— — —	10ft CONTOUR
··· ·········	15ft CONTOUR
———	20ft CONTOUR
⬯	25ft AREAS
✕	GOOD BAIT POSITIONS
●	SWIMS WORTH FISHING AT ANY TIME OF YEAR
◐	GOOD SWIMS FOR CERTAIN PERIODS
🌿	WEEDS
�"'"	SEDGES OR REEDS
🌿	SUBMERGED OR PARTIALLY SUBMERGED BUSHES

Others are fairly shallow with frequent islands and bars where spoil has been left behind in piles as the excavator works through. Really deep pits are only formed where the gravel is in deep seams. The spoil from these pits is usually piled up around the pit and depth variations are less noticeable.

Pike location in shallow pits with many bars and islands is usually a case of finding any more open and deeper areas. Here small fish tend to hole up in the winter and this obviously tends to attract pike. Any small bay which holds a reasonable depth of water is worth investigating. Another worthwhile spot to try is on the ends of long islands or bars. There is a good chance that pike patrol along these bars and being at the end of the bar, particularly casting from the other bank, is a good bet. This type of fishing was first described by Martin Gay and Jim Gibbinson while fishing a variety of South East gravel pits. They caught some very good pike until the waters were filled in and referring back to the articles in the old 'Angling' magazine can be most informative. My best pike from this type of water weighed exactly 26 pounds and came from a slightly deeper area, within a larger area which was also slightly deeper than the rest of the pit. Careful plumbing had revealed this feature and where boats are not allowed I simply walk around after I have finished fishing and cast around with my paternoster tackle, using it to help me plumb the depth. I usually do my first bit of depth plumbing on my first actual fishing visit, unless of course I can do the job properly with a boat. Playing around like this quite often leads the angler to some interesting discoveries. Some other good spots on shallow pits are points where several channels meet, particularly if they are divergent channels. On the edges of islands or on the shelves leading up to the top of bars are all good places to position baits. Here and there on some pits, where the water level has risen and flooded bushes and small trees, pike may be taken in large numbers. Such features are best if they are the only ones in the pit, particularly shallow pits which lack a lot of weed cover. Similarly extensive weedbeds in one area may attract big pike since, although they are not necessarily sitting in the weedbeds, big pike frequently patrol near such areas, because they provide temporary cover for them when stalking nearby food fish.

In deeper pits the pike can be more difficult to locate, for they could be anywhere. Generally, deep pits do not exceed 30 feet—however this does not help us very much for the pike we are after can be in 2 to 30 feet depending on the time of year. Usually the only time the pike will be in the very shallow water will be in March, and then usually if the weather is extremely mild. It can sometimes be worth a cast into such unlikely areas as a friend of mine discovered. He had been sitting blanking with the rest of us and finally as dusk fell he could stand no more, so he cast a livebait into about 3 feet of water and sat down. A short while later he got the shock of his life, when he actually had a run in the shallow water, and quickly netted a 21 pounder! During the spring you can actually watch the pike in such areas and this is a good opportunity to assess the size of pike the pit holds.

For the rest of the year I prefer to fish in water of 10 to 20 feet in depth. Most of my big gravel pit pike have come out of this depth and the time of year does not seem to be that important. The really deep water is always worth a try in very cold weather, but as most of the deep pits I fish in, fish terribly in freezing conditions, this has never really helped me. However, I have had a couple of doubles out of 27 feet deep swims in more favourable conditions, so pike do live there some of the time. The features I try to find in these pits are, I suppose, fairly obvious; points which stick out into the pit, particularly where deep water is within casting range, deep water close in along a bank where the depth is rather less for a good distance, weedbeds close to deep water, and deep water close in, rising to shallower water further out. The biggest problem of all on many pits is that such features are quite numerous, and not all will have pike in residence. Pike being the gregarious creatures they are will frequently be concentrated in one area for a limited period of time. This is not the same as a hotspot, for such aggregations of big pike are very transient. The art of gravel pit fishing is to find these concentrations as they arise, realise when they have dispersed, and then go looking for the next one. The pike move around a lot and do not always favour precise hotspots. These are the holding areas as described earlier which tend to fill up and empty of pike, due to angling or sometimes due to food availability. Most of the pits I fish do not contain enough pike to make a hotspot a viable proposition, so gravel pit fishing has to be an open-minded, mobile exercise.

Luck obviously plays its part in events and this was the case a couple of seasons ago on a medium sized gravel pit. Several of us had been fishing the pit since October and apart from a few doubles nothing much of note had been caught. All the fish which had come out came from the usual swims, fished by all of us for several years now. On one trip Dave Phillips tried a bit of long casting with deadbaits to an area he had previously not bothered with. Imagine his surprise when he landed a brace of 14 pounders — good going on this pit. Unfortunately the distance involved was too much for any conventional livebaiting technique, which was at the time the best method on this water. I had a hunch that by getting as near as possible to the going area and using biggish livebaits, I might just pick up one of the bigger fish, so for the first time I fished the other side of the pit. Ian Greenacre was fishing the usual swim where Dave had had his doubles and by 8 a.m. no-one had caught as usual. I had just sent Kathy home to get a new battery for the van (it expired on the way) when my crucian livebait was grabbed. The fish was running to the right quite rapidly and heading for the other rod. Reeling the other rod in I was ready for action. As soon as I bent into it I knew it was what I had been after, the first ever 20 pounder from the water. Ian came round and took the photos and back she went, 20.14 and a nice clean fish. The next trip was almost a repeat performance, except this time I had two fish. One went 5lb the other 23lb 1oz. Again a largish livebait cast as far as possible to an area about 16 feet deep was the key. The next trip saw a 13 pounder in the net, followed by a 14 pounder next trip. Just before the swim finally died I had two more good fish, in a very short morning session. One took a very large dead trout, and hooked itself on the side of the head, weighing 14.5; the other took a lively little trout livebait and was my fattest pike of the season, 22.05 for 37½ inches.

Whenever anyone fished the usual swim they struggled to catch, and this shows clearly that having the nerve to try new swims can sometimes pay off. Later on that season the other anglers got their own back as some of them found new swims while I blanked!

One of the most interesting features of gravel pits is their varied colouration. Some are crystal clear and when viewed from a distance in sunny weather look beautifully blue, almost emerald green in some cases. Others are coloured with algal blooms, while some are always muddy due to gravel washings entering the pit. One would think that there would be an obvious correlation between water colour and the comparative effectiveness of live and deadbaits. Sod's law as usual says that there isn't! I have fished many crystal clear gravel pits where deadbaits are the number one bait. Similarly I have fished coloured pits where livebaits are as effective as deadbaits. In short, there is no short cut to deciding which approach to use on gravel pits. One phenomenon is very common on pits and this is the situation where very small pike no bigger than 4 pounds outnumber the larger pike in such a way that catching big pike becomes rather difficult. I have fished many such waters and so far I have not really come up with a solution to the problem, which is how to extract the big ones rather than the little ones. Such waters evolve usually because the available prey sizes are either very large or very small. The majority of pike never get beyond the jack

A brace of pit twenties of 21.02 and 22.09, both on deadbaits.

stage, simply because they struggle to find sufficient prey to grow. They are too small to dine on the large prey fish and also suffer themselves from a fairly high mortality rate due to the small population of big pike. The few big ones are the lucky ones, which have at one time or another been able to shoot quickly beyond the jack stage and grow big enough to eat their own kind or the large prey fish. Fishing such waters is very, very frustrating. Deliberately fishing large livebaits is usually hopeless, for the hungry jacks will attack anything a normal pike man will dare to offer. Try using bigger baits and runs on, for instance, jack livebaits, become a monthly event! Legering deadbaits may eventually sort the big ones out, especially if the angler can identify an area where the big fish frequent. This is likely to take a lot of time, so if you commit yourself to this approach you should not take the commitment lightly. The other approach is to fish with small to medium baits and work your way through the little ones. This is generally my approach and I usually also fish one rod with something silly like a big deadbait, more in hope than anything else.

In order to make really big catches of big pike, one usually has to find a big water, perhaps as big as 100 acres. The reason for this is simple. Most gravel pits support a very low biomass of large pike per acre. A high density would be 3 or 4 doubles per acre. Most waters have far less than this and on the big waters you are lucky to have more than one per acre. In order to make a big catch, the water must be very heavily stocked with big pike (usually an artificial situation, see specialised fisheries), or the water must be large with many of the pike located in a very small area. Such concentrations are invariably brought about by pike converging on very big shoals of small prey fish, which can only occur if the water in question is a prolific producer of yearling or slightly older roach, bream or whatever. Therefore not all waters see the pike concentrated in limited areas and on these waters big bags of double figure pike are unlikely. A transient hotspot caused by fry shoals can draw pike from far and wide and the fishing can remain superb until either the fry disperses or the pike finally move away to other areas.

Because gravel pits are generally quite large and fairly exposed, they tend to be affected by wind. While other fish species are very orientated to the direction from which the wind is blowing, pike do not seem to be quite so worried about this. Really strong winds are usually bad fishing conditions on big exposed pits, as the water colours up and drifting weed can make life very difficult. However on really sheltered pits, with plenty of trees around them, I would rate a windy day, with an air temperature of 8 to 15°C as ideal conditions. The first frost usually

The writer's biggest pit pike of 26.10 from Yorkshire. This time the snow didn't put the pike off. It did cure my hangover from the party the night before!

does little to affect big deep pits, in fact on some it can bring the pike on, especially during the afternoon. However, prolonged cold weather slows things down terribly, though I have fished one pit which fishes quite well on really cold days in the middle of really cold spells. In fact on one day in 1981 I had nearly left it too late, but fortunately there was a small corner still free of ice and a 22.15 plus three others was kind enough to oblige and take my smelt deadbaits. Because the pike in gravel pits tend to behave somewhat differently from pit to pit, it pays to come to terms with as many as possible in an area. It is then possible to move to another pit if weather conditions change, or even better, avoid certain waters in unfavourable conditions and fish only those known to 'fish' in the prevailing conditions.

For really big pike, gravel pits provide the pike angler with his best opportunity of catching such a fish. The number of thirty pounders which come from gravel pits each season, probably outnumbers those from all other types of water altogether. Though some of these big fish are caught several times in a season this still means that in some areas there are fair numbers of big pike. However, rather than sitting on a water fishing for a known fish, it is probably better to use a two-pronged approach. By all means put some time in after a known fish, if it is something you really want badly, but do not neglect to try other waters and try hard to break new ground wherever possible. A gravel pit can produce thirty pound plus pike fairly early in its life and many new waters have yielded big fish. By exploring more, the angler is not competing with other pike anglers and I think the satisfaction of having success on your 'own' water is more lasting than that obtained from being angler number 9 to catch Fred the thirty!

f) Lakes, meres and broads

Of all the waters I fish regularly, I rate the large stillwaters termed as lakes, meres and broads as the most difficult. The reason for this is usually the uniformity of the depth and their large size. Some man-made lakes have been constructed by damming small rivers and allowing their valleys to fill with water. The resultant lakes therefore should have a deep end near the dam and a shallow end where the inlet streams or stream runs in. Unfortunately things are not always as clear cut as this and some lakes, such as Coombe Abbey lake, near Coventry, have large areas of uniform depth and very little deeper water. Glacial lakes, such as Hornsea Mere, which were formed by the sheer weight of ice causing a large shallow depression to form. Depth variations are again slight with a maximum of only 8 feet, the rest of the Mere being around 5 feet, and features are few and far between. The Norfolk Broads are perhaps a little more variable. Supposedly the result of peat digging in years gone by, these waters vary from immense sheets of water, such as Hickling Broad, to much smaller waters, often easily overlooked unless you happen to know exactly where they are. Depths again vary, but most are shallow and few are more than 10 feet deep. Of the few I have fished, depth variations and obvious features to guide the angler are so few as to be of no real value to the pike angler.

The first problem with such featureless waters is that what few features there are, are inevitably fished by everyone. If the water happens to be hard fished, then you can bet your life that the likely looking swims have been hammered to death! By likely looking swims I refer to the dam outflow, boat house, the classic reed-lined bay and whatever deeper water happens to exist on the water. So on these types of water the angler may have to try and be original and this invariably requires trying a lot of different areas. Moving about during the day can produce pike, provided they are not feeding during very closely defined feeding periods. (If they are doing this it is possible to be in the wrong spot when they do feed.) On such waters I tend to fish there regularly and try limited areas each trip out. This is slow work, but eventually when you do locate a concentration of pike, you can fish that area and get a lot of big pike in the net during many enjoyable trips. On other types of water the pike are more scattered and may be prepared to take a bait if you can only put one in front of them. This means that the angler has to be prepared to move frequently, as often as every hour. Obviously for this mobile type of fishing a boat is extremely useful and certainly on the Norfolk Broads they are almost essential. I must confess to not liking

Trevor Moss with his biggest loch pike of a shade over 20 pounds. A superb fish for Loch Awe, which does not produce many 20 pound fish. It took a small roach livebait.

boat fishing very much. I tend to feel too confined in a boat and get paranoid if I drop things in the bottom. Before they invented moonboots, my feet used to freeze solid as well (or it seemed that way) on cold days! Despite this I have done a lot of boat fishing and landed one or two good ones in the process. Other writers have described the essentials for boat fishing many times before and the whole thing can get very complicated. Boat fishing should really be put into perspective because of this.

First and foremost you need a boat. You either hire one or buy one. If you hire one you assume that everything on it does not work. Therefore you take your own oars, outboard, rowlocks and anchors! Mcworter's Law says that if anything at all can go wrong, it probably will. Also it is wise to consider a lifejacket, though on very large waters in cold weather you are likely to die from prolonged exposure to the cold as well as drowning. A lifejacket certainly helps your would-be rescuers to find you, dead or alive. I have my own boat, a fairly wide fibreglass job of 10 feet which I can slip on and off a trailer easily enough. I got it second hand for £100 and spent a while painting it and it now looks nearly new. There is certainly little reason to buy a new boat and equally little requirement for a bigger boat unless you plan to fish in company. A 10 footer will run quite nicely with a 3.5 hp outboard and will leave enough room for you, your tackle and the pike! A boat of this size will be safe to take out on most lakes and Broads, but should not be used in really windy weather if there is any doubt at all about its stability.

As far as outboards are concerned, they are a must for fishing large lakes or for running along rivers on the way to the entrances to broads. I do not know very much about outboards, but it seems that Seagulls and Johnsons are favourites. Whenever I use a Yamaha it usually expires on me. On one occasion I filled the petrol tank up with water one dark morning on the Bure, someone having nicked the petrol and left me with water. Needless to say I spent most on the day on the oars! Oars with thole pins are more unwieldy, but easier to use in rough conditions, while oars in rowlocks tend to jump out if you pull too hard, unless you have one of those bars fitted which stop this happening.

For anchoring in shallow sheltered waters, 4 house bricks (the ones with holes) can be tied together, one lot at each end, or you can make proper mud weights out of concrete-filled paint cans. Ropes are best kept short and it pays to tie them to the boat — don't forget to tie the outboard on as well! I do not generally use anchors on such shallow waters, since in order to get them to grip well you need fairly long ropes and in shallow water those are a quick way to lose a fish. Boat rod rests are optional extras and mine were bought from Trevor Moss for £4.60 each. You can do without them quite easily, but having them does help to keep the rods outside the boat, thus giving you a little more room inside.

The most important piece of equipment when boat fishing is some form of padding to prevent damage to the pike, and I usually employ a large sheet of foam rubber. While fishing I use it to sit on, but as soon as I get a run I put it on the boards of the boat. Because I always wear

Boat rod rests are an advantage. This example was supplied by Trevor Moss.

leggings in boats, the foam can get wet, but I can still use it for sitting on. The worst aspect of boat fishing must be clattering about when you are trying to find something. Knives and forceps invariably leap off seats at the first opportunity and will leap in the water if given the chance, with rather final results. It is not easy to get perfectly organised, but try all the same. If Joe Bloggs across the water can hear all the noise, think what the pike might hear! I try to arrange things so that I can reach them from the sitting-down position. It is little use putting things neatly at one end of the boat if you spend half your time climbing about after them.

One of the things I would really like on a fishing boat is a cubby. Think how nice it would be to sit out of the wind and rain, brew up in the warm and generally avoid the boat angler's worst enemy, rain! Until I become more affluent this idea will have to be postponed. If you were really well off a small cruiser complete with cabin might not come amiss; as I said earlier, I don't go fishing to suffer.

Going back to the actual job of fishing lakes, meres and broads, most seem to fish best of all during prolonged mild spells. This was particularly true of Hornsea Mere. Go out on a frosty day and runs were unlikely to say the least. However if the weather had been mild for a couple of days, there was a good chance of a double or two. A good strong wind did no harm at all particularly an easterly which allowed us to belt our deadbaits well into the sanctuary, where the pike seemed to spend a lot of their time. On Hornsea we never saw a sign of prey fish wherever we fished, however on many lakes and broads the distribution of prey fish and the bream shoals can sometimes be established. Dawn and dusk is the time on a calm evening to figure out where the food fish are. It is then possible to try these areas, that or the next day. It does not always work, but if those prey fish seem to favour one area above all other, then there is a chance you won't be far away from the pike.

A strange thing about many meres and broads is that fishing the margins is not always very productive. Frequently it is best to start in the very middle and work in; John Wilson certainly seems to advocate this method and my limited experiences tend to confirm his findings. The margins tend to be very shallow and this is perhaps why the pike are most often located further out. Where reedbeds stand in a reasonable depth of water, say 2 to 4 feet, it is quite possible to extract some very big pike and this was a feature of broadland fishing during the Horsey and Hickling era. Colin Dyson, who as a younger man had pike up to 25 pounds before these waters 'died', reckoned that you had to fish in the reedbeds to catch pike on some days.

My own best day on a Norfolk Broad was the culmination of research, and a series of unlikely events, which eventually led to the capture of a 32.2 pike. Finding the water was the first problem, after some reports of big pike from Norfolk during the previous seasons. The clues were quickly narrowed down and the choice was of two waters, one of which was eventually discarded. The first trip in October was with Dave Plummer, Trefor West and Tony Miles. We fished nearly all day and moved all over the place. Tony got the only fish of 12.6 on half a mackerel just after I had moved out of the swim! For several months I never got around to going back, though Dave had a couple of jack-bashing sessions, and January saw all waters deep in the grip of the freeze-up. However in February everywhere cleared and waters all over the country started to go bananas! One pike angler (whom I will not mention here, because his actions resulted in two dead thirty pound pike) had 6 twenties in a day, so I thought I had better go and try my chosen water, in case it too was going mad. I left an NASG meeting in Quorn earlier than normal, to the words of Trefor West who said it was too late, someone had already caught them! Fortunately both he and I were way off the mark.

Bruno Broughton with a huge Mere pike. It weighed 34¼lb and measured only 43½ inches.

I arrived at the Broad at dawn and found to my cost that I had left my oars at home. There was no alternative but to fish and hope that the long branch I had found would double as a canoe-type paddle. On paddling out, it seemed to be working well, so I headed for an area where I had seen bream rolling in October and where the grebe had fished most of the time. I put on a 10 ounce bream, simply because the bait supply was critical and there were no small ones left. A few minutes after casting out the float was gone and the line was streaming out. I had to leave the fish for a fair while with such a big bait and by the time I struck, my knees were wobbly! It was not as big as I had anticipated, but welcome enough just the same — at 13.02, my first Broad's pike. I fished for another half hour and moved. An hour later I was on the move again, but this time the wind caught me and I could no longer move against it, so that I eventually finished at the end of the Broad in an area where I definitely did not want to be. I thought of abandoning the boat, trying to get back to the van and going in search of some oars, but the boggy nature of the banks put me off the idea. Eventually I found a couple of halved detergent containers which were for bailing out boats. By hanging over the front of the boat it was possible to drag oneself along and eventually get somewhere. I was obviously all in when I finally reached a new spot, casting everything out, and collapsed onto the seat, glad to be fishing again. The peace was shattered by the sight of my red float running back up the Broad. Something had taken my smelt; two runs in a day on a hard water, can't be bad, I thought. Just then the mudweight pulled free and the boat turned round. Somehow I sorted the mess out and hung the net ready for action over the side of the boat, where I was standing. The strike was the usual wind-down and hold it hard affair, and very quickly what felt like a good fish kited halfway round the boat. A tail broke surface and I knew it was a good double, but did not really consider a twenty as a possibility. Once by the boat I noticed the bait hanging along the pike's flank and didn't realise what was going on because I was too busy watching as the pike swam into the net! It was big, big, big! Then the confusion began again, first the hooks and bait were not in the pike's mouth, it had ejected the bait, but the trace (luckily longer than normal) had caught around the back of its jaws. Who needs hooks, I thought, when you can land 'em on a wire trace! So rather than foul hooked, it was not hooked, a strange way to catch your best fish, for that is what it turned out to be. It took the Avons to 32.2, well into the red, the nicest colour of all because it means the pike weighs over 24 pounds. Being such a big fish it was all I could do to handle it and put it quickly into a large micromesh sack I used to use as my landing net. It measured 44 inches, a good length for a thirty. Now, another dilemma, how to get to shore. After a lifetime of struggling with the makeshift paddles I eventually made it. Positioning the pike safely, I risked life and limb and made it back to the car to get Dave Plummer and some oars. I got the oars, but no Dave. Leaving a note, I returned. It was a warm day and I was not very happy about retaining such a big fish for too long, so I took some photos. (I only had 4 shots left between two cameras!) Back she went, full of life and much more likely to survive than a fish which had been messed about. Half an hour later Dave, great bloke that he is, turned up to my profound apologies. Still, perhaps he'll get a thirty next season, hopefully the same one as me, then I'll know that my worrying was worthwhile.

Subsequently I learned that the water I was fishing had not turned up 6 twenties in a day. In fact, as far as I know very little came out that season, so I was obviously very lucky. I paid for it, though. Next day I lost a fish of around 20 pounds on a gravel pit when it dropped off. During the week another twenty got off at the net. To cap it all I landed another pike on the wire trace. Twice in a week, or twice in umpteen years, what odds the same thing happening during one week out of 19 years?

g) Reservoirs

Reservoirs are like gravel pits in one respect—they come in all shapes and sizes. They can be small topping-up reservoirs for canals, such as Welford in Northamptonshire or the famous Tring complex in Hertfordshire. They can be modest water supply reservoirs such as Sywell and Hollowell near Northampton or they can be huge expanses of water such as the 1000 acre plus Abberton in Essex. Most reservoirs are dammed river or stream valleys. Because of this they tend to be deeper at the dam end and shallow at the inflow end. There are exceptions and some reservoirs have been formed by constructing an enormous bowl and concreting or stoning the banks. Somerset's Cheddar Reservoir is such a water. The underwater features of a reservoir depend very much on the geography of the flooded area. Some reservoirs are fairly feature-less due to considerable tidying up work before flooding. Others are flooded without much of this work and the result is an uneven bottom, with the remains of buildings, trees, fences and the old stream bed.

Reservoir fishing is very much a case of learning as much as pos-sible about the depth contours and then fishing all the available features. Once again, the boat angler is in a much better position than the bank angler. With a boat all areas can be covered effectively with live and deadbaits, while the bank angler is restricted to a narrow strip about 100 yards wide, unless he resorts to ballooning baits out. Another unfortunate feature of reservoir fishing is the restrictions imposed on many waters. On Abberton and Staunton Harold reservoirs angling is only allowed from very small lengths of bank. Add to this rod restrictions and one realises that the bank angler is really up against it on such waters. Fortunately these reservoirs can be so good as pike waters, that scratching the surface produces more pike than flogging other waters, so in the end it is all worthwhile. With a free hand the pike angler out in a boat should be able to catch good pike at sometime during the season. Many reservoirs have a handful of big pike and a lot of small ones. The big pike are often up to 30 pounds, but fishing for them can be painfully slow.

Location of such small numbers of pike in, say, a 100 acres of water is the main problem. The more anglers fishing the water, the less likely it is that the usual hotspots will produce the big fish. Such areas include the inevitable valve towers and culverts. However if angling pressure is minimal these are the areas to head for. For most of the summer and autumn, reservoir pike tend to be widespread. The food fish, particularly roach fry, are all over the place and it is not until the winter sets in that massive concentrations of fry start to gather at the dam end and around the valve towers. Once the concentration begins it pays to start pike fishing quick before someone else gets in on the act. However, once the pike have been hammered they tend to make less frequent visits to these areas and certainly on some waters the pike stay well out from the bank. Once this starts to happen bank fishing can be very slow and the best option is to take to the boats if these are available. Alternatively, long range fishing or ballooning can be tried, when conditions are favourable (usually calm or a backwind).

Locating the pike once the usual areas have failed to produce is a time-consuming process. The first step is to fish near the bank, fishing hotspots or holding areas, out of casting range from the bank. Some success will usually be possible. If this area then goes off, the next step is to look for features nearby. Working along trenches or stream beds can be worthwhile as it is quite possible that pike work along these and use them as temporary ambush positions while hunting. Generally I do not take my echo sounder with me when reservoir boat fishing. Instead I plumb the depth around the boat, having selected a likely looking area. If the spot is not suitable I move again, always looking for a feature such as a drop-off. Once located, baits are positioned all round the boat, but always with at least one on the drop-off.

Most reservoirs tend to become very dour in cold weather and none of the ones I have fished have proved productive when ice is starting to form on the water or during periods of strong, cold north easterly winds. Mild weather after prolonged cold spells or the first frosts after mild spells seem to get the pike moving and then is the time to fish long and hard, for the chance of a big pike is never likely to be greater. It was this sort of mild period which led to one of my best catches during one week. It all started with the introduction of the Ravensthorpe pike to Hollowell and ended with three twenties in 5 days. Having caught a brace of twenties at the end of 1978 I had hoped to go on and catch some more big fish, especially as it was the only really good pike water near to Leicester, where I was living at the time. Unfortunately the winter of 1978/79 thought differently and soon into December the temperature dropped and few big pike came out of Hollowell. Things got worse in January with blizzards and a total freeze-up stopping all fishing. Several anglers were waiting for the thaw, which came in early March. Andy Barker was one of them and he managed to fish before me, catching a 28 pounder for his trouble. Monday looked like being my first chance of fishing the water and by this time two twenties had already come from the hotspot. 'Would I be too late?' was the question I asked myself on the way down.

A big reservoir pike swirls powerfully at the net.

I was surprised to find no-one else there and subsequently no-one turned up later so the local grapevine had obviously not woken up to the fact that the reservoir was fishing well. That morning before I drove to Birmingham to work, I caught 4 pike of 22.15, 11.09, 8.04 and 4.00 on livebaits fished in 19 feet of water about 20 yards out on the drop-off. The water temperature was still only 4°C, but the pike were obviously waking up. I could not fish the Tuesday, but Andy did and caught little of note. Wednesday saw me there again, but only a small one had been landed as I packed to leave at about 10 a.m. Fortunately a big pike swirled near one of my floats and shortly after a pike took a small roach paternostered in the usual area. It weighed 26.01 and was a typical 44 inch job, a little lean for the time of year. I motored to work immediately and returned the next day. I was clocking up a lot of miles and Thursday proved a waste of time with only a six pounder taken. This had obviously happened before, a poor day in between two good days, so I resolved to return on Friday and this time Barrie Rickards accepted an invite to give it a try. I half expected him to jam a big one out under my nose! However conditions were the worst I had experienced with big waves blowing right onto the dam wall. It took a lot of effort to get an eight ounce silver bream livebait out to the required area and even more

John Noon with a 22.05 reservoir pike.

John Noon and Pete Haywood with a twenty.

effort to spot the float as it was pounded by the waves. An hour later, after Barrie had missed a few runs, I lost sight of the float, due I thought to drag as the wind increased. However when I got to the rod, line was running out and I quickly hit the fish. Just like all my other big Hollowell pike, the resistance was slight and I do not think that this one even got round to looking the other way, let alone putting up a fight! Barrie netted her and the hooks were extracted easily in spite of the pike having swallowed the bait. She was a fat fish and weighed in at 28¼lb, measuring 42 inches. She was my last big fish that season though I fished there again three more times. The effort had certainly been worthwhile, though how I afforded so many 110 mile round trips while still working each day I will never know. It just goes to show that sometimes one has to be prepared to work very hard for a really good catch of fish—by the end of the season I certainly felt that way!

One feature of reservoir fisheries I have failed to mention is the influence of fry shoals on the feeding habits of the pike. At certain times when small fry are very numerous, reservoir pike can be very difficult to tempt. Even small livebaits in the surface layers can sometimes fail to catch pike which are rolling in your swim. The problem is often that the pike are not really feeding, they are merely active in the surface layers perhaps chasing fry 'for the hell of it' and eating only the odd ones. When the pike are swirling and striking really hard continuously your chances are much better and in these situations almost any well-presented livebait will produce pike.

Where access is restricted the pike may not always be present in your desired swim. I get the impression that on Abberton and Staunton Harold, one is waiting for a pack of pike to move into the small area you are allowed to fish. Because of these limitations sport can be dreadfully slow until the pike move in. From then onwards it can get rather chaotic!

As far as methods and baits are concerned, a key method is the long range legered live and deadbait, using up to 3 ounces of lead to get the bait out. Most waters also respond well to conventional float paternoster tactics and long range half mackerel fishing.

In competitive situations on some reservoirs it is an advantage to cast further than the man next to you. If pike are moving towards the dam, the long caster's bait is likely to be seen by the pike first. Also the long caster can cover far more water. Towards this end some anglers have developed set-ups for increased casting range and there is nothing wrong with this provided the desire does not become obsessive. A few years ago I thought of buying a radio control unit and fitting it to a model boat. I would then be able to tow out my baits further than anyone else.

Unfortunately something or someone got in the way of this scheme. I suspect that other anglers would have fired off a couple of salvos of 3 ounce leads to counter my latest brainwave!

Considering the number of reservoirs in this country, few are available to pike anglers. Many are trout waters and many more are upland waters which are deep and unproductive. As mentioned when I consider trout waters it is a shame that some of these cannot be opened as 'mixed fisheries'. This is unlikely to happen, so for the time being we must make do with the small number of reservoirs available to us.

The smaller fish of the Hollowell brace of 20.09 and 27.00½. The larger fish was my first run on the water. The other gave me the second run.

h) Lochs and Loughs

Spring pike fishing on Loch Lomond.

Of all the waters I fish for pike, the big Scottish and Irish lochs and loughs must rate as the greatest challenge. They also offer in many ways the greatest rewards, few English waters being able to offer the staggering quality fishing of the Scottish and Irish waters. Not living anywhere near these waters does present the average pike angler with a number of problems. For example, I cann₋ t really entertain fishing in Scotland for anything less than a week and this therefore restricts me to holiday visits. These can number only one or two a year, due simply to the expense of fishing away from home for a week. Also one only gets so many weeks' holiday a year! Ireland is even more expensive, due to ferry fares, so one finds the old bank balance is overstretched if one attempts more than two trips a year. None of this will deter the keen pike angler, simply because the quality of the pike fishing is such that the average angler could catch as many twenty pounders in a week as he would during a season of fishing in England.

Like most travelling pike anglers, my first trip to Loch Lomond was a miserable failure. I scrounged a lift with Kevin Clifford and together with Pete and Roger Melbourne, Pete Evans and Erne Colley we spent a very slow week catching two doubles to 11 pounds, plus a few jacks (I had one of the doubles!). We had arrived late March and this proved to be too early, the pike not being present in the bays as we had hoped. Having now fished Lomond several times and also visited Loch Awe a couple of times, I feel that certain lessons have been learned. The most important lesson is that of when to fish the big lochs. For most of the year the pike are out in the relatively deep water, compared with the margins, around the 10 to 25 foot mark. Only during the spring are the pike to be found regularly in shallow water of less than 6 feet. Because the shallow areas are generally relatively small compared with the rest of the loch, the pike tend to be concentrated during the spring, compared with other times of the year. The pike enter the shallows initially prior to spawning and this can be from any time in late February onwards. Once they have spawned, usually during the end of March or early April, the pike stay on the shallows awaiting the other coarse fish which use the same shallows. Perch generally move onto the shallows in late April and the members of the carp family follow later in May. As mentioned earlier, during the post-spawning period the pike feed heavily on the other fish as they run in to spawn and obviously as they leave the spawning grounds, suitably knackered! So, not only are the pike concentrated in certain areas, they are also feeding hard. This is why the spring is the loch fisherman's most productive time for pike. Several times in the past I have read that fishing at this time of the year is unsporting and unfair because the pike have not had time to recover from their efforts. Some even suggest that spring pike fishing is about catching spawning pike. All this is nonsense and anyone who has actually done any spring pike fishing would agree. For a start the pike, though lean, are far from out of condition. The fast runs and tail walking are almost as spectacular during the spring as during the summer. Nearly all my spring pike have been very clean fish, quite solid and very nice to look at. Spring pike fishing is not catching spawning pike. The reason for this is simple, pike do little feeding before and during spawning. Try fishing for them too early in the spring and a blank is on the cards. Some pike appear to spawn twice, but your only chance of catching them would appear to be in-between spawning, not while they are doing it for the second time. The biggest contradiction of all is the fact that at least two of the greatest critics of pike fishing during the spring have killed between them over half a dozen twenty pounders. I'll let the reader decide who is the real sportsman!

Loch pike fishing outside of the spring bonanza period is a different affair altogether and entails seeking the pike out in the deeper water, but let's first look at the problems associated with fishing on the shallows during the spring. On both Irish and Scottish lochs we are looking for shallow areas of not more than 10 feet in depth. Sometimes depths of as little as 2 feet will produce very big pike so it pays to keep an open mind as to the likely pike holding areas. Most of the shallow bays or areas are near to where large rivers run into the loch. On Loch Lomond the River Endrick has built up an extensive shallow area with associated shallow bays. Most of the Endrick Bank, as it is known, is sandy and less than six feet deep. Here and there, particularly in the bays, is to be found limited weed growth. A similar situation exists at the northern end of the loch where the River Falloch has produced a large weedy bay and associated shallows which extend a short way out into the loch before dropping off to depths in excess of 200 feet. In Ireland similar bays exist, but generally they are much more weedy and often the water is a peaty brown rather than crystal clear as on Lomond. To catch pike during the spring it is important to locate these areas and reference to any good map will provide useful reference points. Such areas are frequently littered with sunken trees and branches washed down by the floods, so the approach by boat has to be cautious to say the least. A broken shear spring or pin on an outboard can mean a long row home. Also while fishing these areas it is wise to try and ascertain the location of snags for

Remarkably calm water on Loch Lomond, looking south from Ardlui.

no line that exists will get you out of trouble if a pike takes and gets the line caught under a snag.

Whenever possible I try to bank fish these shallow areas, mainly because of my dislike of boat fishing. Bank fishing is so much easier, especially when it comes to handling the pike. However if you intend to bank fish, waders are essential, for it is usually necessary to wade a good distance before the bait can be cast out into a reasonable depth of water. Thigh waders are all right for most jobs, but I prefer chest waders. Using these, extra distance can be obtained and in heavy rain they are the ideal 'leggings', keeping body and soul completely dry. In chest waders you can sit, kneel or fall over and still stay dry. Care has to be taken when wading as sunken obstacles are easy to stumble over, so it pays to wade by lifting one's feet well off the loch bed. Once or twice when wading, pike have almost been trodden on, and I remember well Andy Barker's reaction recently, when he nearly stepped on a good double. Fortunately a few minutes later he had a really good tearaway take on half mackerel and duly landed a beauty of 24lb 6oz, but it is still worth remembering that pike do come in very close and a spooked pike will not always take a bait. So wade when required, not by habit! Spring

Pete and Roger Melbourne and Pete Evans head out onto Lomond for another blank!

Trolling equipment in Ireland. Large boat, Seagull outboard and trolling rest.

pike fishing in Ireland mainly involved the use of deadbaits as live-baiting is banned in the south due to fears over the spread of roach to new waters. So far this has presented few problems to visiting pike anglers for the Irish pike are very keen on deadbaits. This is very nice, simply because the hassle of bait catching and lugging them around is eliminated. Irish pike are receptive to lures and wobbled deadbaits, so there are alternatives to livebaits if required. The pike of some of the Scottish lochs are different. Though it is possible to do very well on Lomond and Awe using deadbaits, I have known periods when livebaits were essential to catching any numbers of pike. It is therefore wise to ensure that a good supply of bait is at hand. Two of us needed nearly a hundred baits for one spring trip when we caught over 60 pike.

Bank fishing with deadbaits is a fairly simple matter provided certain rules are remembered. In some situations a 40 yard wade, followed by a 60 to 70 yard cast will see the bait over 100 yards from the bank. Plenty of line is therefore required. I find that my Mitchell 410 spools will hold ample 15 pound Sylcast for this work, easily 150 yards. My Cardinal 55 is also very suitable for this type of work. There is no need at all for bigger reels of the fixed spool or multiplier type. Extending rod rests are essential for they usually have to stand in a couple of feet of mud and water. I usually keep the rod tip well up and use a small pilot float to help keep the line off the bottom. This is obviously not totally effective as the weight of a 100 yards of line causes a big bow which must obviously touch the bottom. However, when one winds in or strikes into a pike, the float helps the line come up quicker and also shows where exactly the pike is heading. For livebait fishing, standard float paternoster gear is employed. On certain lochs, such as Loch Awe where few snags are encountered, I scale down to 11lb line for livebait fishing as this allows longer casting. If you like boat fishing there is no reason why you should not use this approach. It certainly lends itself to a mobile approach and using a boat gives you a much greater choice of swims. Nearly all spring pike fishing requires the use of a boat to reach the shallows and even if you do not boat fish, the boat can be a handy place to keep all the tackle, especially in boggy areas.

Last spring (1982) Andy Barker, Barry Kerslake and myself were fishing again in Ireland. The receding water levels made fishing rather difficult, with a long walk through marshy margins to dry land. To save a lot of splashing about we often used the boat as a base for bait, tackle and cameras, thus avoiding having to cart everything to shore. One spot

Andy Barker again with a leaping 19 pounder.

we picked was very boggy for quite a long way out and the three of us plus my wife (who had to be piggy-backed to the shore!) squeezed into the bay as best we could. By this stage of the holiday I was getting fed up with sitting in quagmires, and my bait casting was inspired by very little confidence. An hour after casting out Barry attracted our attention in no uncertain a manner by declaring that a big pike had rolled about 60 yards out. I think we decided that Barry had been on the vitamin G again (Guinness) for though we all stood up to look around, none of us expected to see any signs of fish. A few minutes later we were still scanning the water when my attention just happened to fix on one of my floats. Just then a dorsal and tail fin broke surface and something moved by the float. Seconds later the float itself moved and then the buzzer sounded. I had actually witnessed a pike stand on its nose in 2½ feet of water to pick up the smelt deadbait. Needless to say I hit the fish which had by now moved close to Andy's rod on the left. Using as much force as possible I tried to turn the fish away from his line. Unfortunately all my pulling did not really make much impression on the fish, it simply kited in, until it was over Andy's line and about 10 yards out. Eventually I got its head round and had it on the way to the net. We all got a good look at a craggy head and a fair length of body as Andy tried to get the net under it. She was not having any of this and half jumped out of the water as she ran a short distance. She soon responded to increased pressure and in no time was in the bottom of the net. *!!!**!! or something like that, either way it was pretty incoherent. Andy knew it was a big one simply because he had felt its weight in the net. Laid out in the larger of several puddles it was clear that this fish would go over 28 pounds. Kathy looked pleased, Andy looked pleased and I don't know what Barry was thinking except when he uttered strange phrases in what seemed like the local dialect. We weighed her and she went well into the red, 26, 27, 28, 29, 30 (wow!), 31, 31.12, 31.14 with the tail off the ground. Cheers all round or was it words like 'The jammy sod has done it again!'. Either way, this time I got some decent photographs and before releasing it we obtained a measurement of 46½ inches, a very big fish, likely to top 34 pounds when in spawn.

While it is quite true that we would have fished just as effectively from a boat it is obvious that three or four of us would have required more than one boat, so bank fishing even in a bog is easier, less expensive and leaves you less disorganised after landing the odd thirty pounder. The choice of swims is perhaps the biggest problem facing the pike angler while fishing the shallows. Generally when fishing bays, you are well advised to fish well into the bay, the far end being a good choice.

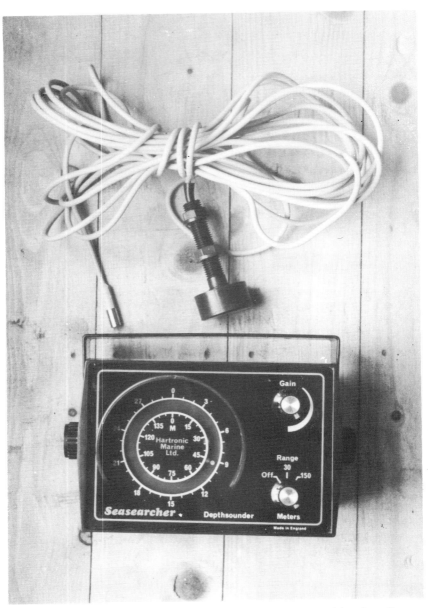

Hartronic Sea Searcher Depth-sounder, box and transducer. Can be either dry cell or car battery powered.

On some lochs it seems that the pike move into the bay, failing to feed until they are well inside. Trying to ambush them on the way in does not always work! Such movements can happen very quickly. A bay which seems devoid of pike can come to life very quickly with many pike landed in a short space of time. Sometimes the pike swirl on the way into the bay and such surface activity can be the prelude to some good fishing. In my experience surface activity is seldom conducive to pike sport. I have tried crazy crawlers, deadbaits and in desperation even the landing net to catch such fish! Both Andy Barker and myself have had good fish follow plug baits fished on the surface. One big fish did an impersonation of Jaws behind a crazy crawler before continuing to roll and swirl through our swim. The first evening of our 1981 trip saw only one 8 pounder landed despite a lot of surface activity. Next day from 11 onwards three of us had five doubles, the best two of 19.02 and 27.14 to my rods. It appeared that some big pike had moved in, but were not yet ready to feed. Next morning they commenced feeding. It may be that these pike were spawning and switched onto the feed after finishing their duties; however in 1982 something happened which suggested to me that pike get up to some funny behaviour after they have spawned. Barry had tried to tempt what appeared to be two pike which had been swirling on the surface and eventually got one, a 13 pounder. As Andy landed it a 4 pounder jumped into the net after it! The 13 pounder was certainly too lean to be a contender for spawning, so why had it acquired such a devoted consort? Perhaps spawning behaviour continues after the act? Either way the situation has to be noted as it can result in some very frustrating fishing. Usually when loch pike are really on the feed you see little surface activity. This was the case in 1979 when Kathy and I made our last trip to fish Lomond. We drove up overnight and motored out to the bay and were fishing by 10 a.m. No-one else in sight, the ideal situation! Despite fishing in only 3 to 4 feet of water, each take came without warning. I think about 11 fish had been landed including a couple of low doubles and I was sitting with spaghetti bolognese on my lap when at about 6 p.m. a small roach livebait was taken. I struck and was not surprised to be met with a decent amount of resistance. What did surprise me was the way the rod slammed down as the pike made three short runs of about 10 to 15 yards, resulting in it putting another 40 yards between it and the bank. It then did a bit of kiting and tail walked. They always look smaller when you are playing them so as usual I had no real idea of its actual size. Once in the net it was soon realised that my previous Lomond best would have no chance against this one. At 44 inches and 26 pounds, she was probably the nicest looking pike I have

24lb Irish pike taken on long range half mackerel in shallow water.

Irish Action! On the right you can just see a 24.06 pike throw the whole mackerel out.

ever had. A few weeks later it made John Watson's day when it turned up at 24 pounds. (I suspect this fish to be one which spawned twice, for it was certainly not fat when I caught it.) The last couple of runs produced a small one and a 15.15 at dusk and provides a good example of what to do when a pike gets into a snag. This pike had run to the left very quickly preventing me from getting a good angle on the fish·to steer it away from a large tree which lay in the water. It was snagged so I went to get the boat rather than try pulling. As I started to get into the boat, the pike moved out of the snag and I had to run back and resume battle. On other occasions the boat has enabled me to free snagged lines and even lift out half trees! My other Lomond twenty of 20lb 1oz was landed from a boat after it had run through dense weedbeds. Never try brute force, always use the boat. Nine out of ten times you will get the pike out. Better still is to avoid letting the pike get into the snag. While boat fishing you might get away with strong-arm tactics; however, when bank fishing between snaggy areas, strong-arm tactics are fatal. It is far better to ease off the pressure on a big fish and allow it to swim out into open water, rather than pull it kiting into a snag. The only time to bully a pike in such swims is when you know that you have the advantage on the fish. Again chest waders are a boon for one can wade out past many obstructions, enabling trouble-free landing of pike.

Sometimes during the spring, the pike temporarily move off the shallows, and then it pays to try out in deeper water near to the shallows. I think it was April of 1978 when I learned this lesson the hard way. I caught very little on the shallows while two other blokes moved out onto the drop-off on the Endrick Bank and proceeded to land some superb pike, topped by a 26 pounder. Similar situations prevail in Ireland and it pays to be willing to try deeper water if the shallows are producing little. Fortunately the pike usually return to the shallows thus making location much easier.

My experience of loch fishing during the summer and autumn is rather limited, but enough has been learned to enable some success to be achieved. On the Irish loughs trolling is the accepted method and is without doubt the best method to use when the pike are out in deeper water. Here an echo sounder can be used to advantage enabling set depths to be trolled effectively. The aim is generally to fish around the 20 foot mark, though pike may be picked up in deeper and shallower water. George Higgins' account of his biggest Irish pike gives an insight into trolling methods as practised by Irish anglers and requires little additional comment from me. My trolling has been mainly with dead-baits and artificial lures, and deadbaits have generally outfished lures, though I am sure every method has its day. Deadbait trolling is fairly simple and entails trolling any small to medium sized bait behind the

TROLLED DEADBAIT

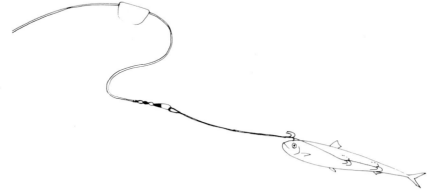

IN THIS CASE A SMALL MACKEREL. TRIO OF TREBLES, SIZE 8s. FOLD-OVER LEAD WEIGHS ½-1 OUNCE — ELIMINATES KINK AND KEEPS BAIT DOWN. BAIT DOES NOT SPIN BUT EITHER RUNS STRAIGHT OR REVOLVES VERY SLOWLY.

boat, using the outboard for propulsion. One aims to run the bait without wobbling; it appears that a bait run straight is most effective. Generally I prefer to hold the rod and feel for a take, giving line on feeling a pike grab the bait. This is fairly unmistakable as snags simply bend the rod round while pike give much less resistance and can be felt to move with the bait, i.e. they are for a few seconds pulled along. It is essential to give line before the pike lets go. My best trolled pike of 21.12 nearly didn't get hooked, simply because after an unproductive morning's trolling I presumed that I had snagged bottom when in fact it was a big pike. I pulled to free the bait and the pike pulled back. Luckily one of the three trebles on the trout deadbait took hold and after a really epic battle she ended up in the net.

Trolling can be much more specialised than I have indicated and anyone who feels he ought to learn more about it should read some of Fred Wagstaff and Bob Reynolds early writings. Lead core trolling lines for getting baits down to 20 or 25 feet may have their uses, but because this style of fishing is outside my experience the reader would do well to consult the previously mentioned authors.

It has been said many times before that the big waters can be dangerous to fish. I am, I suppose, a fairly carefree type, however I do

Paul O'Dwyer with an Irish walking tree. Actually, roots like this are formed because of the changes in water levels experienced on some Loughs.

not take chances when out on lochs. You must have a lifejacket for each angler, in the boat. You can get away without wearing it during good weather, but as soon as things start to look rough, wear it! Rapid changes for the worse are a feature of both Irish and Scottish weather and my advice to the would-be loch angler would be this: never go out unless you can handle a boat. Never go out if rough weather is forecast. Always know where the best areas of sheltered water are. Always have oars, a baler and a reliable outboard. If you do get caught out, try and keep heading into the waves and either make for a sandy shore (beware of rocky shores, they sink boats), and beach the boat and wait for better weather or head for shelter or home. I've been scared more than once and I do not intend to risk my life for the chance of a big pike; instead I would rather find another smaller water or river to fish from the bank.

Bank fishing on lochs can be productive provided deep water can be found close in. Terry Eustace and Roger Baker showed that it was possible to do very well on deadbaits from the bank during October in Ireland. Following in their footsteps I have found that bank fishing is a useful alternative when trolling is dour. After spending 3 abortive days on the troll during October of 1981 I ended up bank fishing and duly landed a 24.14 on half mackerel. However bank fishing can be deadly slow, until pike move into the swim. The trouble is that it can take a week for the pike to move in. Life is too short to tolerate more than 3 blank days!

Finally before George Higgins tells his own story, what about the prospects of a giant pike from the lochs? Well, though Lomond has produced some very big fish including Slim Baxter's 34¾lb beauty and another of just over 35 pounds, I still do not rate Lomond as a mega-pike producer. All the records suggest that Ireland is the place to seek out the giant pike. Waters such as Lough Mask have produced so many 35lb plus pike, even in the light of the slaughter by gill nets, that this water must rate as a potential 40 water. Loughs Allen, Ree and Derg are also very good candidates for a 35 pound plus fish and if I were to try and beat my personal best, it would be one of these waters which I would try. Having had a couple of thirty pounders my ambition now is to catch one a little bigger. In time, provided I continue to visit Ireland I feel that I will have a chance of getting a personal best and though I'm not expecting a 35 pounder, if it comes along one day I won't be complaining!

AN IRISH THIRTY

by George Higgins

August was three weeks old and three days of blissful isolation, with a little pike fishing thrown in for good measure, lay ahead of fellow piker Larry Nixon and I. As boat fishing addicts the 20 square miles of water at our disposal gave us lots of scope. We avoid other anglers even at the expense of ignoring favourite swims and apart from a brief encounter with a jolly little Frenchman we had the place to ourselves. Mock sympathies were expressed to the little man who had lost a big pike the previous day when his finger-hold in its eye sockets failed. He understood our anger sufficiently to equip himself with a big net that very day which he waved to us in the afternoon.

Any aspirations we may have had about catching a very big pike were no more than those which perpetually draw us back to the lough like a magnet. One hundred and thirty days spent there in six years have taught me a lot. I have learned to accept defeat—often, but I never despair and as long as the bait is in the water I'm in with a chance. The last cast of the day can be just as thrilling as the first.

August is a month not usually associated with big catches but the pike are lean and mean as hell. Airborne acrobatics are not uncommon.

Trolling from a powered or rowed boat, depending on wind conditions, is our choice and anyone who dubs it a monotonous pursuit has not done it correctly. So much is happening that at times three hands would be an asset. Not least in its favour is the thrill of the hunt, the anticipation on approaching a favourite lie and the sheer heart-stopping suddenness of the strike.

The reaction of a speeding pike on slashing a trolling bait is worlds apart from that taking a legered bait and I know which thrills me most.

This first day was soft. A gentle ripple ruffled the surface along the densely wooded shore and the grandeur of the surrounding mountains accentuated our isolation. Larry settled for a single rod but could easily have managed two. 'Copper Alexanders' are a finely made home bashed piece of domestic copper pipe shaped to traditional copper spoon lines by fellow club member Alex Dickey. Alex's spoons have caught more 20 pounders than all our other artificials put together and Roy Smyth has used them for years with devastating effect. Larry and I selected one each and I put out a second rod baited with frozen perch.

A ghillie's life is terribly hard and doing the honourable thing I gave Larry first refusal of the only three hungry pike in the lough, failing myself to 'get a rise'. His first strike was vicious from a heavy pike which threw the spoon high in the air as it displayed its broad flank before making good its escape. The second strike made history for Larry whose face changed from ashen white to crimson and all the shades in between. I reckon that pike played Larry for a full fifteen minutes before it was hoisted aboard, a beautiful unblemished specimen of 23¼ lbs and Larry's best. The third and last pike of the day weighed a little over 5lbs.

Day two was overcast with a light south east wind. We were caught napping on the east shore when the wind dropped suddenly and just as quickly sprang up from the west, blowing hard within minutes. We battled our way westwards, pounding through two miles of treacherous waves with spray breaking over the bow until we reached the comparative tranquillity of the western shore. I invited Larry to play a hunch. A year previously, in the same area where Larry caught his big pike and at exactly the same time, 2 p.m., I caught a pike of 23½lbs. Returning the following day at exactly the same time, I got one of 22½lbs. (Not the same pike.) We arrived fifteen minutes early and on the first run along the edge of the sunken island Larry's spoon was snatched by a real scrapping specimen which gave a comparable performance to the 23 pounder but faster. It weighed in at 18¼lbs. Three smaller pike made up the day's catch.

Boat fishing makes one restless for new pastures and on the third and final day we changed direction and fished at the opposite end of the lough some four to five miles distant. By noon Larry had a 5¾lb pounder, and lost a possible double when on exploding wildly into the air it threw the spoon defiantly several yards. I had strikes from two pike, missing them both. Then for no reason that I can explain, other than divine providence, I did a strange thing. Having completed several tacks past a favourite mark I turned the boat quite suddenly and without warning, through 90°, much to Larry's annoyance for a tangle of trolled lines seemed inevitable. Diving into my tackle bag I came up with a rather tarnished ABU Copper Ellipse spoon. In what can best be described as frantic haste my trusty but until now fishless Copper Alexander was reeled in. On went the Ellipse to be cast back over my shoulder and swallowed up in the wake of the boat.

Larry looked puzzled. 'Have you ever caught anything on that thing?' he asked. 'No', I said, 'but I'm going to.' Larry's wry smile had barely faded when with a jarring thump the lure struck something solid. Any resistance is always treated with respect but this looked like bottom except that this bottom took off. I shouted 'fish' to Larry, and throwing the boat hard to starboard gave the throttle a burst, heading upwind. The sheer unyielding mass of this pike indicated something special.

When the boat stopped moving forward after cutting the motor, Larry flung the anchor far into the wind and reeled in the spare rod. It's wise to put as much distance as possible between the pike and the anchor; let battle commence. I stood up. At that very instant the heavens opened and rods of solid rain, or so it seemed, transformed the scene into a set for a Hammer Horror movie; waves flattened under the onslaught as a grey mist enveloped the surface. Water and sky became as one. Beneath all that a pike acted out the principal role in this drama, sending shock waves to the rod tip and unmercifully dragging line from an hysterical reel. The long runs to all points of the compass became shorter and more confused until at last the pike lay deep below the boat. I bent the rod as much as I dared but it would not budge and I knew that this was the biggest pike I had played for a very long time.

I desperately wanted to catch a glimpse of it but when it set off on another long run and the line raced up towards the surface, I instinctively sunk the rod tip and applied all the side strain I could muster. The last thing wanted at this stage was a leap and the inevitable head shaking, thrilling as the spectacle would have been. Disaster was averted and the pocked surface of the water boiled. Several minutes and a lot of persuasion later we looked down on the broad back of a pike of great length. Larry had kept silent vigil, net in hand, awaiting his cue.

'This is my biggest pike', I said, which on reflection can't have made him very happy about the part I expected him to play. First attempt to net it missed and it shied away beneath the boat, surging deep and stripping line against the clutch. Second time round there was no mistake, the netting was done beautifully. Larry had repaid his debt in full. Together we hoisted this great hulk aboard. As if to herald the fact, the rain stopped as suddenly as it had appeared. The black clouds rolled back and we were bathed in warm sunshine.

Twenty-six years of piking and there at my feet, perfect in every detail, lay the biggest pike I had ever seen in the flesh. Inside its great toothy maw I found the little twist of copper, the catalyst that brought us together, nestled with one hook of the treble lying limply round the root of the first gill raker. No penetration, no damage, I just lifted it out. How close had I come to losing it had it jumped? I dread to think.

It weighed in at 30½lbs, later amended to 30lb 6oz, and measured 46 inches to fork of tail, a potential 40 pounder come March. Alas, it would not have been capable of the battle it had just lost and it was with great pride that it was slipped gently into the water to disappear with a few powerful strokes of its great tail.

Only a better pike can ever displace your best. Larry has since achieved that goal but I am confident that it will not take another 26 years for me to do the same.

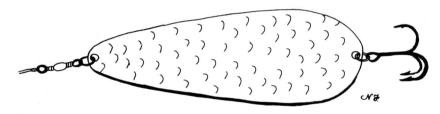

copper Alexander

George Higgins with his 30lb 6oz Irish pike. ▶

i) Trout waters and artificial pike waters

A book on modern pike fishing would not be complete without a mention of the role of trout fisheries and artificial pike waters in today's pike fishing scene. All over the country trout waters exist and continue to be created. Some have a pike population and these waters are worthy of the pike angler's attention. Sadly many trout waters are not open to the pike angler, despite experiments at various waters which suggest that pike angling does little if any damage to trout stocks. There are other valid reasons for not allowing pike fishing on reservoirs in particular. Foremost is the cost of allowing pike anglers to fish our large reservoirs. The amount of work required to maintain boats and ensure effective bailiffing of pike anglers may not be covered by the income obtained. Another reason is that pike fishing may rapidly decline due to the removal of the pike, thus making the operation of only a short term nature. However, is it essential to remove the pike? I have long hoped that some trout reservoirs could be dual purpose, managed as trout and pike waters. I am sure that the extra revenue from pike anglers would cover the extra trout needed to replace losses. Unfortunately, none of the Water Authorities are forward thinking enough even to consider such an approach. I do not think anyone has even tried to cost such an exercise. The quality of the pike fishing would be staggering and it is possible that anglers from other countries would travel to fish such a water. A relatively small reservoir of 100 acres would probably support 20 to 30 pike over twenty pounds plus 60 or 70 double figure fish. The trout would provide the extra feeding and imagine the number of pike men who would flock to catch two or three twenties or a dozen doubles in a day. I would certainly be prepared to pay a decent amount for a day ticket, probably the same price as a trout ticket. During the trout season pike anglers could be restricted to certain areas or a close period enforced. This is all a bit of a dream, but one day I hope it will become reality.

At the present time the pike angler tries to fish any trout water he can. He knows that there is a chance of some very big pike and also it is possible, providing the correct consents are obtained, to transfer those pike elsewhere. Trout waters are rapidly fished out so it is essential to fish them early on in their pike producing career. I fish a couple of trout waters which have been well and truly hammered and consequently seldom catch anything. However I will continue to fish them, simply because of the slim chance of meeting up with a mega-pike! A low pike density and unlimited food is likely to produce not just thirty pound pike, but big thirty pounders. It pays not to fish too hard on a hammered water, simply because the big pike may be non-existent. The odd trip is all I am prepared to devote to such waters, the rest is down to luck.

Trout water pike are frequently very fat and obviously well fed. Because of this they often require more attention to detail when fishing for them. Deadbaits are frequently poor producers and I have found that good sized livebaits such as chub are required to tempt the pike. They seem to be preoccupied with large food items so it is a good idea to offer a quality bait. Runs can also be finicky with dropped runs and missed takes a possibility. The best time to fish for trout water pike is usually when water temperatures are still fairly high, i.e. in the autumn or as they rise in the spring. The back-end has another advantage, as many of the trout will have died, been eaten or been removed by the trout fisherman the previous season. The pike might be a bit hungrier, giving the angler a better chance. It is vital when fishing trout waters not to bend the rules; nobbling the trout is definitely out. You are there to catch and hopefully to save the pike. Getting banned for the price of a few trout is not worth it and it reflects badly on the pike man.

Artificial pike waters are still very rare. Some have been a success, others less so. Bill Chillingworth's Woolpack fishery was one of the first, but was initially overstocked leading to the pike going back in condition. Hollowell Reservoir was stocked with at least a dozen twenty pound plus pike when Ravensthorpe Reservoir was drained. At the time food fish stocks in Hollowell did not appear to be sufficient to support such big pike, but fortunately things seem to have settled down and some nice pike have been caught. Recently some Rutland Water pike have gone in and these seem to have done quite well. Ideally an artificial pike water should be overstocked with pike and artificial feeding used to keep the pike in good condition. This is best done by introducing stunted or unwanted fish from other waters. Smaller artificial pike waters can be fed during the season with fish offal from the local fishmonger. Severn Trent Water Authority has considerable experience of running a purpose-built pike water. At Kingsbury Water Park near Birmingham a stocked pike water has performed quite well in spite of an initially low prey to pike density of 4 to 1 by weight. The biggest problem facing anybody wishing to open an artificial pike water is getting the fish. It is wrong to steal other people's pike for your own waters so pike have to come from where they are unwanted. There is certainly no need to kill and sell big pike these days as there are a number of waters which can be stocked with such fish. Generally artificial pike waters are less likely to produce really big pike, due to the high density of pike. However as far as fun fishing is concerned, they certainly make good waters for catching quantities of pike. After spending a lot of blanks after a big fish it is nice to be able to retire to a prolific water and actually get some runs.

It has been predicted before that trout waters will produce the next 40 pound pike. I would agree with this suggestion, with the following qualification: the chances of a 40 pounder are greatest from big trout waters which are not intensively culled during their early days. Pike densities are low and the pike have a chance to grow large. Few waters fit this bill, but watch out if someone starts pike fishing on a big virgin trout water.

N.J.F.'s Pike over 20lbs.

32.02	Norfolk Broad	Smelt deadbait	FL	Feb 82
31.14	Irish Lough	Smelt deadbait	FL	Apr 82
28.07	Lincolnshire Pit	Half herring	L	Feb 83
28.04	Hollowell Reservoir	Bream livebait	FP	Mar 79
27.14	Irish Lough	Perch deadbait	L	Apr 81
27.00½	Hollowell Reservoir	Rudd livebait	FP	Dec 81
26.10	Brandesburton Pit	Rudd livebait	FP	Jan 77
26.01	Hollowell Reservoir	Roach livebait	FP	Mar 79
26.00	Lincolnshire Pit	Smelt deadbait	L	Jan 83
26.00	Loch Lomond	Roach livebait	FP	Apr 79
26.00	Notts Gravel Pit	Sardine	FL	Mar 82
25.14	Notts Gravel Pit	Roach livebait	FP	Dec 82
25.13	Lincolnshire Pit	Sardine	L	Dec 82
25.04	Lincolnshire Pit	Smelt deadbait	L	Jan 83
25.04	Lincolnshire Pit	Sprat	L	Jan 83
25.04	Irish Lough	Roach head	FL	Apr 81
25.01	Lincolnshire Pit	Roach deadbait	FL	Jan 83
24.14	Irish Lough	Half mackerel	FL	Oct 81
24.14	River Delph	Crucian livebait	FP	Nov 73
24.08	Norfolk Broad	Half herring	L	Feb 83
24.02	Lincolnshire Pit	Smelt deadbait	FL	Jan 83
24.00	Irish Lough	Half mackerel	FL	Apr 81
23.13	Fen Drain	Smelt deadbait	L	Nov 82
23.13	Lincolnshire Pit	Sardine	FL	Dec 82
23.12	Relief Channel	Rudd deadbait	FL	Sep 74
23.09	Lincolnshire Pit	Half mackerel	FL	Nov 82
23.05	Lincolnshire Pit	Half herring	FL	Nov 82
23.04	Loch Lomond	Roach deadbait	FL	May 82
23.01	Norfolk Gravel Pit	Chub livebait	FL	Nov 80
23.00	Relief Channel	Dace livebait	FF	Nov 68
22.15	Notts Gravel Pit	Smelt deadbait	L	Feb 81
22.15	Hollowell Reservoir	Roach livebait	FP	Mar 79
22.09	Notts Gravel Pit	Sprat	FL	Feb 82
22.08	Fen Drain	Whole herring	FL	Dec 77
22.08	Relief Channel	Roach livebait	FF	Nov 73
22.07	Notts Gravel Pit	Smelt deadbait	FL	Feb 82

22.05	Notts Gravel Pit	Half mackerel	FL	Feb 82
22.05	Hollowell Reservoir	Crucian livebait	FP	Sep 79
22.05	Norfolk Gravel Pit	Trout livebait	FP	Nov 80
22.04	Relief Channel	Herring head	FL	Sep 74
21.14	Relief Channel	Half mackerel	FL	Feb 74
21.13½	Norfolk Gravel Pit	Bream livebait	FP	Nov 81
21.12	Irish Lough	Trout deadbait	T	Aug 80
21.10	Relief Channel	Smelt deadbait	L	Mar 70
21.08	Notts Gravel Pit	Smelt deadbait	FL	Nov 82
21.06	Relief Channel	Whole herring	FL	Mar 71
21.05	Lincolnshire Pit	Sardine	FL	Dec 82
21.04	Fen Drain	Half mackerel	FL	Dec 79
21.02	Notts Gravel Pit	Roach deadbait	FL	Feb 82
21.02	Norfolk Broad	Roach livebait	FF	Mar 83
21.01	Lincolnshire Pit	Smelt deadbait	L	Jan 83
21.01	Notts Gravel Pit	Crucian livebait	FP	Sep 82
21.00	Relief Channel	Whole herring	FL	Feb 68
21.00	Irish Lough	Half mackerel	FL	Oct 82
21.00	Relief Channel	Whole mackerel	L	Feb 70
21.00	Mill Basin Drain	Roach livebait	FP	Dec 71
20.14	Norfolk Gravel Pit	Crucian livebait	FP	Nov 80
20.11	Norfolk River	Half mackerel	FL	Nov 74
20.09	Norfolk River	Smelt deadbait	L	Dec 80
20.09	Hollowell Reservoir	Roach livebait	FP	Dec 78
20.08	Relief Channel	Roach livebait	FP	Dec 70
20.08	Relief Channel	Dace livebait	FP	Sep 72
20.06	Irish Lough	Half trout	FL	Apr 81
20.05	Roswell Pit	Rudd deadbait	L	Mar 77
20.04	Notts Gravel Pit	Half mackerel	FL	Oct 82
20.04	Relief Channel	Dace livebait	FF	Oct 68
20.04	Fen Drain	Roach livebait	FP	Mar 75
20.02	Notts Gravel Pit	Roach livebait	FP	Feb 82
20.01	Loch Lomond	Half pike	L	May 77
20.00	Norfolk Gravel Pit	Roach deadbait	FL	Dec 73

Key

FL Float leger; FP Float paternoster; L Leger; T Trolled; FF Float fished

References

Normally references will have previously been mentioned in the text. This is not the case here, additional references having been included here for the interest of the reader. Most, if not all, are either current books or periodicals available on loan from the British Library, Lending Division, Boston Spa, Wetherby, LS23 7BQ. For out of print books it is worth trying R. I. W. Coleby, Chapel House, Louth Road, East Barkwith, Lincoln LN3 5RY, a supplier of second-hand books.

ALLEN, J. R. (1939) A note of the food of the pike (*Esox lucius*) in Windermere. J. Anim. Ecol. *8* (1): 72-75.

BOUQUET, H. G. J. (1979) The Management of Pike Stocks. Proc. 1st British Freshwater Fish Conference. 176-181.

BULLER, F. (1971) Pike. Macdonald.

BULLER, F. (1979) The Domesday Book of Mammoth Pike. Stanley Paul.

BULLER, F. (1981) Pike and the Pike Angler. Stanley Paul.

FICKLING, N. J. (1982) The identification of pike by means of characteristic marks. Fish. Mgmt. *13* No 2, 79-82.

FROST, W. E. & KIPLING, C. (1959) The determination of the age and growth of pike (*Esox lucius*) from scales and opercular bones. J. du Conseil Perm. lit pour L'Expl. de la Mer. *24*, 314-341.

FROST, W. E. & KIPLING, C. (1967) A study of the reproduction, early life, weight-length relationship and growth of pike in Windermere. J. Anim. Ecol. 36: 651-693.

GAY, M. (1975) The Beginner's Guide to Pike Angling. Pelham.

GAY, M. (1978) Pike from Pits and Lakes. In 'The Big Fish Scheme'. Ed: F. Guttfield, Benn.

GIBBINSON, J. (1974) Pike, Osprey Anglers Series.

JOHNSON, L. (1966) Experimental determination of food consumption of pike for growth and maintenance. J. Fish. Res. Bd. Can. *23*: 1495-1503.

KIPLING, C. & W. E. FROST (1969) Variations in the fecundity of pike in Windermere. J. Fish. Biol., *1*(3): 221-227.

LAWLER, G. H. (1965) The food of the pike, in Hemming Lake, Manitoba. J. Fish. Res. Bd. Can. *22*(6): 1357-1377.

MAITLAND, P. S. (1977) Freshwater Fishes of Britain and Europe. Hamlyn.

MANN, R. H. K. (1976) Observation on the age, growth, reproduction and food of the pike in two rivers in Southern England. J. Fish. Biol. *8*, 179-197.

MAUCK, W. L. & COBLE, D. W. (1973) Vulnerability of some fishes to Northern pike predation. J. Fish. Res. Bd. Can. *28*: 957-969.

RICKARDS, B. & WEBB, R. (1971) Fishing For Big Pike. A. & C. Black.

RICKARDS, B. & WHITEHEAD, K. (1976) Plugs and Plug Fishing. A. & C. Black.

RICKARDS, B. & WHITEHEAD, K. (1977) Spinners, Spoons and Wobbled Baits. A. & C. Black.

SPENCE, E. F. (1928) The Pike Fisher. A. & C. Black.

Useful Addresses

ALAN BROWN, 118 Nightingale Road, Hitchin, Herts.
ANDY BARKER SPECIALIST FISHING TACKLE, 16 Loweswater Road, Binley, Coventry, W. Midlands, CV3 2HJ.
ANGLERS CO-OPERATIVE ASSOCIATION, Midland Bank Chambers, Westgate, Grantham, Lincs. NG31 6LE.
DAVE BARNES, (Specialist Umbrella Tents), 21 Northdown Park Road, Margate, Kent.
DELKIM DEVELOPMENTS, 27 Lea Road, Benfleet, Essex, SS7 5UU.
DELLAREED LTD, 20 Eagle Hill, Ramsgate, Kent, CT11 7PY.
GARDNER TACKLE, Hullbrook Farm, Shamley Green, Guildford, Surrey.
GUDEBROD, Masterline U.K. Ltd, Cotteswold Road, Tewkesbury, Glos., GL50 5DJ.
HELIN TACKLE COMPANY, Detroit, Michigan, 48207, U.S.A.
JAMES HEDDON and SONS, Dowgiac, Michigan, U.S.A.
KEN LATHAM, Potter Heigham, Gt. Yarmouth, Norfolk.
LAZY IKE CORPORATION, Fort Dodge, Iowa, U.S.A.
MULLARKEY & SONS, 184/185 Waterloo Street, Burton-on-Trent, Staffs., DE14 2NH.
KEVIN NASH, Happy Hooker Products, 5 Silverdale, Rayleigh, Essex.
NATIONAL ASSOCIATION OF SPECIALIST ANGLERS (formerly N.A.S.G.), Sec. Des Taylor, 20 Grampian Road, Stourbridge, West Midlands, DY8 4UE.
NORMAN MANUFACTURING CO. INC., 2910 Jenny Lind Road, Fort Smith, Arkansas 72901, U.S.A.
PIKE ANGLERS CLUB, Sec. John Watson, 173 Moore Avenue, Sprowston, Norwich, Norfolk.
SIMPSONS OF TURNFORD, Nunsbury Drive, Turnford, Broxbourne, Herts.
SKEE-TEX LTD, Battlebridge, Essex, SS11 8TR.
TERRY EUSTACE RODS & TACKLE, 2a Booths Lane, Great Barr, Birmingham.
TREVOR MOSS (The Tackle Shop), 42 Tooley Street, Gainsborough, Lincs.

Pike Fishing Bibliography

I have included here what I believe to be the hundred or so most informative and most interesting writings on pike which have appeared in the various magazines since 1967. Obviously I have overlooked some significant articles; however, a read of all those included here should be more than sufficient for even the keenest pike angler. There have been some excellent series in the weeklies such as Anglers Mail, particularly the 'School of Pike Fishing' which ran in the late sixties. I have not included them here simply because I was foolish enough not to keep them. They remain for me a memory!

E. Allen	CA	Feb 79	Rainbows End in Giant Pike
R. Baker	CFM	July 81	Pike on the Troll
A. Barker	CF	Nov 79	Livebait Action & Method
A. Beat	CA	Nov 80	The Green Lagoon
S. Cheshire	CF	Feb 79	Feeling for a Drain
B. Church	CF	Nov 80	Piking on Lough Allen
A. Clark	F	Oct 67	They Really Do Like 'Em Big
K. Clifford	CF	Feb 77	To Have or Have Not
K. Clifford	CF	Nov 77	The Real Truth About Loch Lomond
C. Dyson	CA	Oct 77	Broadland Past
C. Dyson	CA	Mar 81	Death of a Legend (Dennis Pye)
T. Eustace	A	Oct 77	Pike Hunt 1
T. Eustace	A	Nov 77	Pike Hunt 2
T. Eustace	A	Dec 77	Pike Hunt 3
T. Eustace	A	Jan 78	Pike Hunt 4
T. Eustace	A	Dec 78	Another Pike Hunt 1
T. Eustace	A	Jan 79	Another Pike Hunt 2
T. Eustace	A	May 79	Belly Up Pike
N. Fickling	A	Dec 72	Piking on Fenland Drains
N. Fickling	A	Oct 73	Collecting & Keeping Livebaits
N. Fickling	A	Sept 74	A Plethora of Pike
N. Fickling	A	June 75	Pike Hotspots & Feeding Periods
N. Fickling	A	Aug 75	1974 Piking Lessons
N. Fickling	CF	Jan 76	Winter Piking
N. Fickling	CF	Nov 76	Pike Cycling?
N. Fickling	CF	Mar 77	The Growth Rate of Pike
N. Fickling	CA	Sept 77	Better Deadbaiting 1

N. Fickling	CA	Oct 77	Better Deadbaiting 2
N. Fickling	CA	Nov 77	Better Deadbaiting 3
N. Fickling	A	Feb 78	Take Good Care of Esox
N. Fickling	A	Mar 78	Spring Pike on the Shallows
N. Fickling	CA	July 78	Is Leapfrogging Overrated?
N. Fickling	CA	Dec 78	Methods, You Need Them All
N. Fickling	FW	May 79	Hooks for Predators
N. Fickling	A	Oct 79	Odd Pike
N. Fickling	CA	Nov 79	Only When the Sun Shines
N. Fickling	CA	Jan 80	Pike Fishing in Small Rivers
N. Fickling	CA	Apr 80	It's Time to Blow the Gaff
N. Fickling	A	Jan 81	The Hollowell Myth
N. Fickling	CA	Aug 81	Holiday Pike Bonanza
N. Fickling	CA	Dec 81	Facts and Fantasies
N. Fickling	CA	Feb 82	Big Pike Waters, Hunger is the Key
N. Fickling	CA	Apr 82	Analysis of Pike Baits
M. Gay	A	Jan 70	Thoughts on Pike Runs
M. Gay	A	July 72	The Care and Ultimate Preservation of Pike 1
M. Gay	A	Aug 72	,, ,, 2
M. Gay	A	Sept 72	Hotspots, Their Value to the Pike Angler
M. Gay	A	July 73	Lures and Sport Fishing
M. Gay	A	Feb 74	Deadbait Dodges Again
M. Gay	A	Sept 74	Proof of the Pudding
M. Gay	A	Oct 74	Trouble Free Pike Paternosters
M. Gay	A	Jan 75	The Pleasure of Piking
M. Gay	A	Oct 75	Pike Hotspots
M. Gay	A	Nov 75	Heavyweight Pike
M. Gay	A	Jan 76	Pike Fishing Firsts
M. Gay	A	Mar 76	Knock 3 Times
M. Gay	A	Feb 77	Those Pike That Drop the Bait
M. Gay	CF	Apr 78	Comment (Lomond debate)
M. Gay	CA	Feb 79	Bite Indicators for Pike
M. Gay	CA	Mar 79	Pike Traces
M. Gay	FW	Mar 79	Abberton Awakes
S. Harper	A	Aug 77	Float Trolling a Neglected Art
B. Harris	A	Dec 74	The Leapers of Lough Allen
G. Higgins	F	Oct 69	The Pike of Lough Beg
J. Gibbinson	CF	Oct 78	Pike Odds and Ends
R. Gibbinson	A	Aug 74	You Live and Learn

B. Jackson	CF	Sept 80	Plug Fishing for Pike
G. Marsden	CF	Apr 76	Scots Piking
M. McEwan	A	May 80	Big Pike in Ireland 1
M. McEwan	A	June 80	Big Pike in Ireland 2
M. Mousley	CFM	Nov 81	Fast River Pike
J. Nolan	A	Sept 73	Live/Dead Cocktails for Choosy Pike
D. Phillips	CF	Mar 80	Successful Piking
D. Phillips	CF	Apr 80	Pike Location
D. Phillips	CF	Nov 80	Giving it the Lot 1
D. Phillips	CF	Dec 80	Giving it the Lot 2
D. Phillips	CF	Mar 81	Deadbaits, Some Lessons Learned
D. Phillips	CF	Dec 81	The Long & Short of Piking
D. Plummer	CF	Sept 76	Loch Lomond Pike
D. Plummer	CF	May 77	Lomond Revisited
D. Plummer	CF	Apr 79	Piking on Lomond
D. Plummer	CF	Apr 81	The Road to Lomond
D. Plummer	CF	Mar 82	Winter in Norfolk
B. Reynolds	CF	Feb 81	Greased Line Live and Deadbait Fishing
B. Reynolds	CF	Apr 81	Deadbait Spinning for Pike
B. Reynolds	CF	May 81	A Matter of Choice
B. Rickards	CF	Dec 80	Pike Killing—the Big Con.
J. Sharratt	CF	May 80	Fight for Survival of Gassed-up Pike
G. Stapylton	CF	Mar 78	Repetitive Pike
G. Stevens	CF	Jan 82	Pike Hotspots
D. Steuart	A	Nov 74	'Pikes'
D. Steuart	A	Dec 74	Pike on the Paternoster
D. Steuart	A	Mar 75	How Many Dead Pike is One Dead Pike
D. Steuart	A	Oct 76	Reservoir Pike
P. Stone	A	Nov 73	Deadbait Dodges
J. Watson	FW	Apr 79	The Promise of Loch Lomond
J. Watson	CF	Oct 81	Three Days in December
R. Webb	CF	Jan 78	Pike Fishing—My Story
R. Webb	CF	June 80	On the Road Again
J. Wilson	A	Jan 77	Broadland Pike After Prymnesium
J. Wilson	CA	Oct 77	Broadland Present

Key to angling publications:

A	=	Angling
CA	=	Coarse Angler
CF	=	Coarse Fisherman
CFM	=	Coarse Fishing Monthly
F	=	Fishing
FW	=	Fisherman's Weekly

INDEX